# Japanese Aircraft

RECOGNITION
HANDBOOK

**RESTRICTED**

The Naval & Military Press Ltd

*Published by*

**The Naval & Military Press Ltd**
Unit 5 Riverside, Brambleside
Bellbrook Industrial Estate
Uckfield, East Sussex
TN22 1QQ England

Tel: +44 (0)1825 749494

www.naval-military-press.com
www.nmarchive.com

*In reprinting in facsimile from the original, any imperfections are inevitably reproduced and the quality may fall short of modern type and cartographic standards.*

# FOREWORD

The contents of this Handbook have been derived from many sources. All silhouettes were redrawn by J. G. Moore, W.R.N.S., from bromide prints prepared and flown out by D.A.R. Mat. Ministry of Aircraft Production. Photographs are mainly from the School's collection supplied by M.A.P. together with suitable ones copied from Intelligence publications from all areas. Performance figures were likewise from these sources, notably JAF/6A produced by Int. 5 Air Command S.E.A. and T.A.I.C's Summaries. Where possible these are corrected for local atmospheric conditions.

Information in the text, extracted from Secret or Confidential sources, has been suitably modified for inclusion in a Restricted publications.

G. C. T.

East Indies Station,
Aircraft Recognition School,
Trincomalee, Ceylon.

21st October, 1944.

# JAPANESE AIRCRAFT
# Recognition Handbook

### LIST OF CONTENTS

1. PREFACE.

2. REVISION OF JAPANESE CODE-NAMES.

3. BOMBERS.

    | | | | |
    |---|---|---|---|
    | BETTY | Navy | 1 | T.E. T/B Land based. |
    | FRANCES | Navy | | T.E. T/B. D/B Land based. |
    | HELEN | Army | 100 | T.E. B. and Reconnaissance. |
    | JILL | Navy | | S.E. T/B Carrier borne. |
    | JUDY | Navy | 2 | S.E. D/B. Reconnaissance. |
    | LILY | Army | 99 | T.E. Light B. and D/B. |
    | LIZ | Navy | 2 | F.E. T.B. |
    | KATE | Navy | 97 | S.E. T/B. |
    | NELL | Navy | 96 | T.E. T/B. |
    | SALLY | Army | 97 | T.E. B. |
    | VAL | Navy | 99 | S.E. D/B. |

4. RECONNAISSANCE.

    | | | | |
    |---|---|---|---|
    | DINAH | Army | 100 | T.E. R. Land Plane. |
    | EMILY | Navy | 2 | F.E. R. Flying Boat. |
    | JAKE | Navy | 0 | S.E. R. Floatplane. |
    | PETE | Navy | 0 | S.E. R. Floatplane. |
    | MAVIS | Navy | 97 | F.E. R. Flying Boat. |

5. FIGHTERS.

    | | | | |
    |---|---|---|---|
    | IRVING | Navy | 2 | T.E. F. and reconnaissance. |
    | NICK | Army | 2 | T.E. F. |
    | OSCAR | Army | 1 | S.E.F. and light D/B. |
    | RUFE | Navy | 2 | S.E. Float F. |
    | TOJO | Army | 2 | S.E. F. |
    | TONY | Army | 3 | S.E. F. |
    | ZEKE 22 | Navy | 0 | S.E. F. Carrier borne. |
    | ZEKE 32 (HAMP) | | 0 | S.E. F. Carrier borne. |
    | ZEKE 52 | | 0 | S.E. F. Carrier borne. |

6. TRENDS IN JAPANESE DEVELOPMENT, AND NEW AIRCRAFT.

# JAPANESE AIRCRAFT
## Handbook for East Indies and British Pacific Fleets

INTRODUCTION.

This handbook is not intended in any way to replace B.R.150, which is the standard Naval Manual of Aircraft Recognition, in being a complete reference book on important operational aircraft. Nor is it intended to cover preliminary instruction in the subject. A need was felt, however, for a handbook of Japanese aircraft, which could be used mainly as an up-to-date basis for instruction, but also as a bridge reference book. As it is produced locally it can be amended more easily than one printed in the United Kingdom. Only information necessary for good recognition and good gunnery, i.e., salient characteristics and useful performance figures, are included, together with the latest distribution and operational areas of the various aircraft types. This latter information, it must be realised, changes with the fortunes of war, so is given in broad outline only.

2. Again, giving only certain information, this handbook in no way replaces E.F.I.S., which is an intelligence and not a training publication, and as such has much detail quite irrelevant to recognition and a completely different emphasis on the subject of aircraft. E.F.I.S. with a smaller distribution than these notes, which are intended for class consumption, is of much higher security grading.

3. With still only few intact Japanese aircraft in Allied hands, silhouettes are being revised constantly as new facts come in. Those contained in this handbook are as accurate as it is possible to draw with the knowledge available, but they will be amended as soon as more exact information makes it imperative for new drawings to be produced.

4. Ideally too, flying photographs of views normally seen by naval gunners should be included, but such is the scarcity of good flying "shots" that any view available is better than none at all and is, therefore, included. Those unsuitable ones, i.e., top views, will, it is hoped, be replaced as soon as other views materialise.

AIDS TO RECOGNITION.

5. Aircraft recognition is aided considerably by an informed interest in the enemy's whereabouts and the forms in which he exists and operates. Periodically C.A.F.O.s are published (the latest being C.A.F.O. 830/44) giving "order of sighting lists" in the main battle areas. A sound knowledge of what to expect from the enemy, during an operation in any given area, gives confidence to the look-outs and imbues the close range gun's crews with the right aggressive spirit for the occasion. Recognition Officers can be of immense help by putting up on notice boards, rough sketch maps of the area in which the operation is to take place, marked in different colours, each representing the operational zone of the different enemy aircraft expected in the area. This will draw attention to the importance of remembering or noting the *operational radius* figure of the different types, for by so doing, one can reduce the relatively large number of operational types which may be seen, to a comparative few. This number increases, of course, as one approaches the enemy held coast, but knowing what to expect and when to expect it, is half the battle and is just another way of "being in all respects prepared to meet the enemy." This point together with the appreciation of the need to remember roughly the dimensions of the various types for range estimation, and *sea level* speeds, for estimation of aim-off in close range weapons still without gyro-sights, rather than the more exciting and glamorous maximum speeds usually attained at altitudes out of reach of close range weapons, helps to impress upon one the fact that aircraft recognition is not a purely academic subject practised by a select few, but is of vital practical importance to accurate close range gunnery and fire control.

MATERIAL.

6. Make a point of seeing the C.A.F.O. on "Recognition of Aircraft-Training Organisation and Training Material" and getting what is due to your ship. (The latest is C.A.F.O. 1076/44 cancelling C.A.F.O. 1282/43). Training material has been produced in many parts of the world,

some good, some bad—all is of value provided its limitations are realised. The essential point to remember is that old material will almost certainly be inaccurate. Therefore, keep in your library of silhouettes and books, only the latest available, and discard ruthlessly—if only old information is available, mention the possibility of changes to your class. With aircraft models it is rather more difficult, but some stores models which are slightly inaccurate, may be trued up from silhouettes and photographs. This applies to some of the first metal models produced in India and now becoming available to the East Indies Station through naval stores. Furthermore, once silhouettes have been finalised, very satisfactory models can be made from them. It should be remembered that a coat of paint covers a multitude of sins!

INSTRUCTION.

7. Instructions should follow the general plan laid down in B.R.150, (The Naval Manual of Aircraft Recognition) the very comprehensive preface of which will not be enlarged upon here. Mention should be made, however, of a common mistake made by instructors, namely when working through the W.E.F.T. system, it is applied to each of the three views, head-on, plan and side, in turn. This results in the class thinking of the aircraft *as seen in those three* views, whereas they should have a general impression of the aircraft in their minds from which they can deduce how the aircraft will appear in *any* view. Do not stick too closely to the description of the silhouette on paper. Try to get the class to think what it would look like in the air a long way off. A training device which will help the class to attain this, is the shadow-graph.

DEVICES.

8. On board there is little room or time for elaborate training devices and two of the most simple and effective are the blackboard and the shadow-graph. Sketching on the board induces increased observation of detail for the sketches to be accurate; whilst the shadow-graph (using the beam of a ciné projector to throw the shadow of a model on to a ground glass, oiled paper or taut sheet screen) teaches the class to appreciate the transition from silhouette to flying view, and with practice teaches them to convert automatically the silhouette into the solid—to think in three dimensions. Don't become a gadgeteer. Make and use only those devices which are really useful and demonstrate certain important points, for it is better to rely upon a few good ones than many inferior ones.

PROPORTION.

9. A further point to be stressed during preliminary instruction is the importance of *proportion*. The difference in proportion of similar objects of everyday life is usually taken for granted. Who, for instance, would confuse a greyhound with a dachshund?—yet broadly speaking it is only proportion which makes them different dogs! Between, for example, two twin engined aircraft, there are not only vast differences possible in the positioning and shape of the main features, wings, engines, fuselage and tail unit, but the sizes of each feature in relation to one another—*i.e.*, their relative proportions—can differ so greatly, that identification is possible, once those proportions are appreciated, at a range long before detail itself becomes apparent; certainly long before the markings are visible, let alone identifiable. The unconscious appreciation of proportion, together with the sit of the plane, lies at the back of all "snap spotting," so necessary and effective during a sortie into enemy waters.

TACTICS.

10. The principles behind all methods of attack are dealt with in the preface of B.R.150, whilst those especially applicable in this theatre of war are described, with examples, in E.F.I.S. JA/4100,/4101,/4102. It *must* be remembered that it is the *general principle* and not the example which should be understood and remembered by the look-outs and close range gun crews. By knowing what type of attack is possible from the aircraft spotted, correct fire distribution can be carried out to counteract the tactics dictated by the local conditions prevailing at the time—visibility and cover, both natural and artificial.

11. In the near future it is likely that more torpedo attacks will be made on shipping; more dive bombing will be carried out by aircraft other than VAL, *e.g.*, JUDY, FRANCES and possibly LILY. Low level bombing by fighters may well increase and extend to shipping targets.

SECURITY.

12. It might be noted here that the security aspect of the subject should be stressed to all classes. Because of the limited reconnaissance facilities of the aircraft industry of Japan, only now possible, mostly through Super Fortress raids, knowledge of new Japanese aircraft types must come from "sources" inside that country. Should information reach the enemy, through careless talk on the part of any enthusiast on the subject, that certain details of new machines are known to us, the enemy will know where, amongst the technicians, the man who could be responsible for the "leak" might be and our Intelligence would lose that flow of knowledge. This would be unfortunate even though total cover of Japan's aircraft industries were possible.

INTEREST.

13. Finally—instruction should be made something more than just the imparting to a class, the shapes, speeds and bomb loads of aircraft. Try to find a story or a piece of information about each plane which will fix it in the minds of the class, giving that plane a personality of its own. There are two schools of thought about such interest, one beginning, the other ending with it. Both are successful. Choose your own method. Never be afraid of repetition; it is as well to repeat the facts three times, presenting the same fact differently each time. Don't forget that "three light taps will drive the thinnest nail into the thickest wood"!!

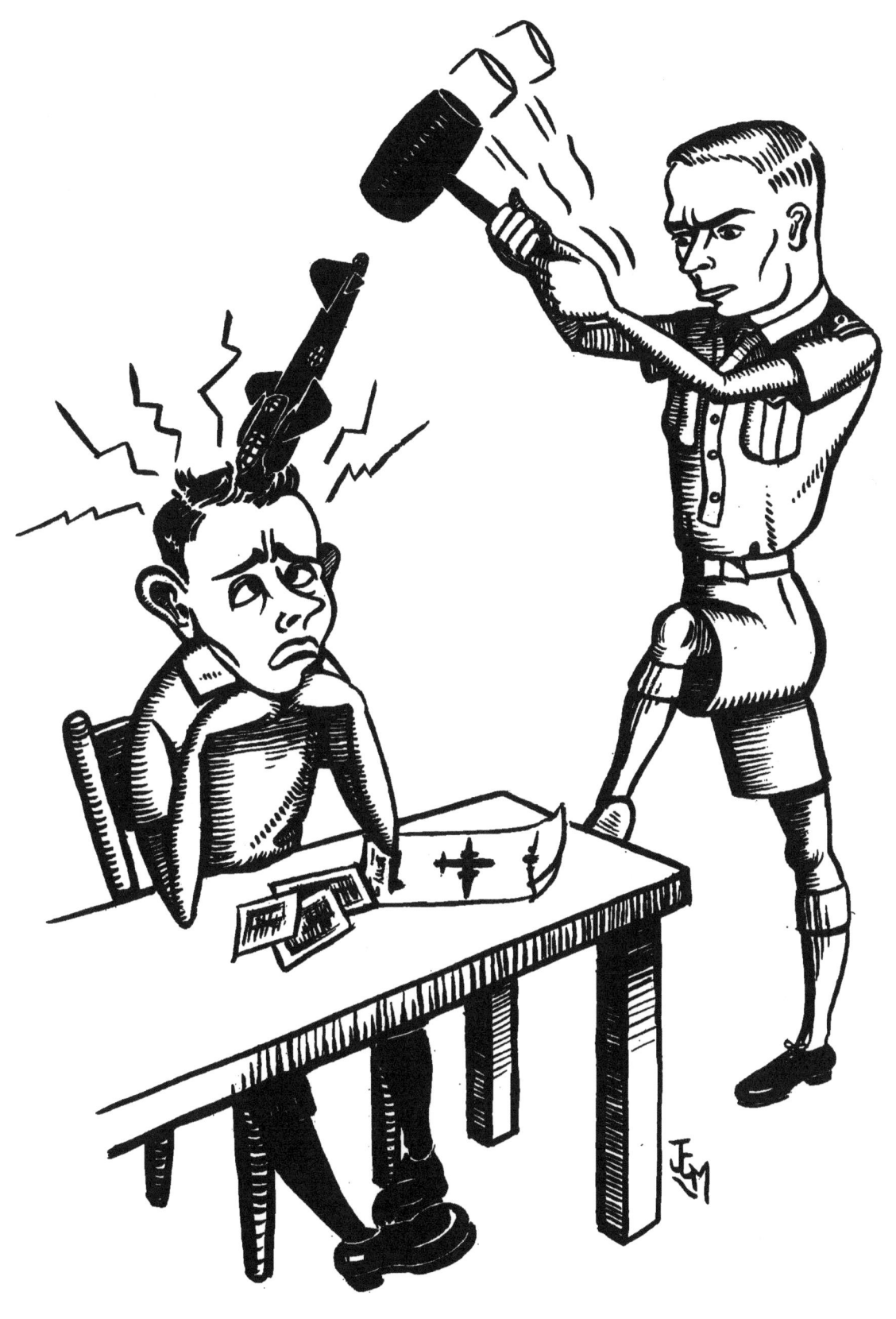

"THREE LIGHT TAPS _____"

## REVISION OF JAPANESE CODE-NAMES

The main change brought about by a revision of Code-names, decided upon by the Technical Air Intelligence Centre, Anacostia, D.C., U.S.A., is that all Mark numbers will be dropped entirely and in their place, the Japanese Model number, given to each version of an aircraft as it comes into service, will be added to the existing S.W. Pacific Code-names—thus ZEKE 52 or EMILY 12 or HELEN 3. No change occurs in the full official descriptive title which combines

(1) Service to which the aircraft belongs—Army or Navy.

(2) Last digit or digits of the Japanese year number.

(3) Description of type of aircraft, e.g., single engined Fighter, twin engined Bomber, etc.

There are two types of Japanese Model Numbers—the Navy using a two digit number and the Army a single digit number.

In the Navy, as each new *type* of aircraft becomes operational, it is given the Model number 11—really 1.1. The first digit represents the airframe and the second the engine installation. For each structural alteration of the airframe made in subsequent *models* the first digit of the Model Number is changed and if the engine is replaced by a different type, the second digit is altered. In this way the evolutionary changes in a particular type of aircraft can be followed and the potentialities of a new model of that type can be judged largely from its Model Number.

An example of the changes occurring in a basic type can be shown in the evolution of the Navy O. Carrier borne Fighter whose Code-name is ZEKE. The original service model now obsolete, was given the Model number 11. Thus the full Code-name under the revised scheme would be ZEKE 11.

| *Code-name/Model Number* | *Airframe Changes* | *Engine Changes* |
|---|---|---|
| ZEKE 11 Original Model | Fixed round wing tips | Sakae 12 |
| ZEKE 21 | *Folding round wing tips* | Sakae 12 |
| ZEKE 22 | Folding round wing tips | *Sakae 21* |
| ZEKE 32* | *Square tips, reduced span* | Sakae 21 |
| ZEKE 42 | Did not become operational | |
| ZEKE 52 | *Round tips, reduced span* | Sakae 21 |

*ZEKE 32 when first reported was treated as a new type because of its short wings with square tips and thus was given a different Code-name HAMP, whereas it was merely ZEKE 22 with the folding tips removed. To bring this aircraft into line with the rest of the story of ZEKE's development, the name HAMP is to be dropped and the aircraft referred to, logically, as ZEKE 32.

Nothing has been heard of the next airframe alteration and ZEKE 42 has never been operational. This absence of a complete series of model numbers is on a par with the gaps in the Mark numbers of the Spitfire.

The Army Model Number System is less accurate in its working and refers mainly to airframe changes, thus giving a less complete picture of each type's evolution, than the Navy's two digit system.

It will be realised that for recognition purposes, this revision of Code-names will make little difference, with the exception of the dropping of the name HAMP (or HAP). When considered from an Intelligence point of view its importance will be seen, but little stress should be placed upon the subject of Model Numbers when referring to them in class. Only sufficient to enable the class to appreciate the reason for the changes, and what is to be deduced from them, should be discussed.

It can be taken that performance figures given in this handbook are for the latest model in large scale use.

**BOMBERS**

SPAN 82'4"  **BETTY**  LENGTH 65'6"
BOMBER

Eastern Fleet Chart Production Unit.

# "BETTY"

## NAVY 1. TWIN ENGINED LAND BASED TORPEDO BOMBER

CHARACTERISTICS.

Mid-wing monoplane with very marked dihedral from roots of equally straight tapered wings, with narrow blunt tips.

Two underslung radial engines in long cowlings.

Long deep glazed nose, long deep streamlined fuselage ending in glazed tail cone gun position.

Broad-based low tail fin/rudder, wide-spanned, narrow tail plane set in front of gun position.

CREW.

5—7.

DIMENSIONS.

Span 82'4". Length 65'6".

SPEED.

Maximum. 285 knots at 20,000 feet.
230 knots at sea level.

OPERATIONAL RADIUS.

Maximum. 1,600 miles as reconnaissance and shadower.
1,100 miles with 1,760 lb bomb/torpedo.

BOMB LOAD.

Normal load 1 × 800 kg. (1,760 lb) bomb or torpedo.
Common load 12 × 60 kg. (total 1,784 lb).

ARMAMENT.

1 × 7.7 mm. machine gun in Nose, Lateral (2) and Ventral positions.
1 × 12.7 mm. machine gun or 1 × 20 mm. cannon in large Dorsal Turret amidships.
1 × 20 mm. cannon in Tail.

NOTE.

Important as torpedo aircraft replacing NELL. At first disappointing, later models have more powerful engines and may, therefore, be faster than given speed. Armament is not standard, later models being minus lateral blisters and with large dorsal turret placed over after wing root, and tail cone truncated to increase arc of fire of tail cannon. There are many new models, the performance figures above are for Model 22 and may even be improved upon in still more powerfully engined ones, the latest of which is "bullet proof." Fuselage modifications in the latest model are rounded wing-tips, slight alteration to tail plane, taper and tips.

Sharp dihedral on relatively long wings, and deep but narrow fuselage are differences between BETTY and the MARAUDER (seen mostly in S.W. Pacific) which has fat circular fuselage and high placed, short, flat wings and a tail plane with dihedral. WARWICK and WELLINGTON have, in proportion, much shorter fuselages which are deeper and blunter, due to true turrets in nose and tail and have very tall fin/rudders as opposed to BETTY's squat one.

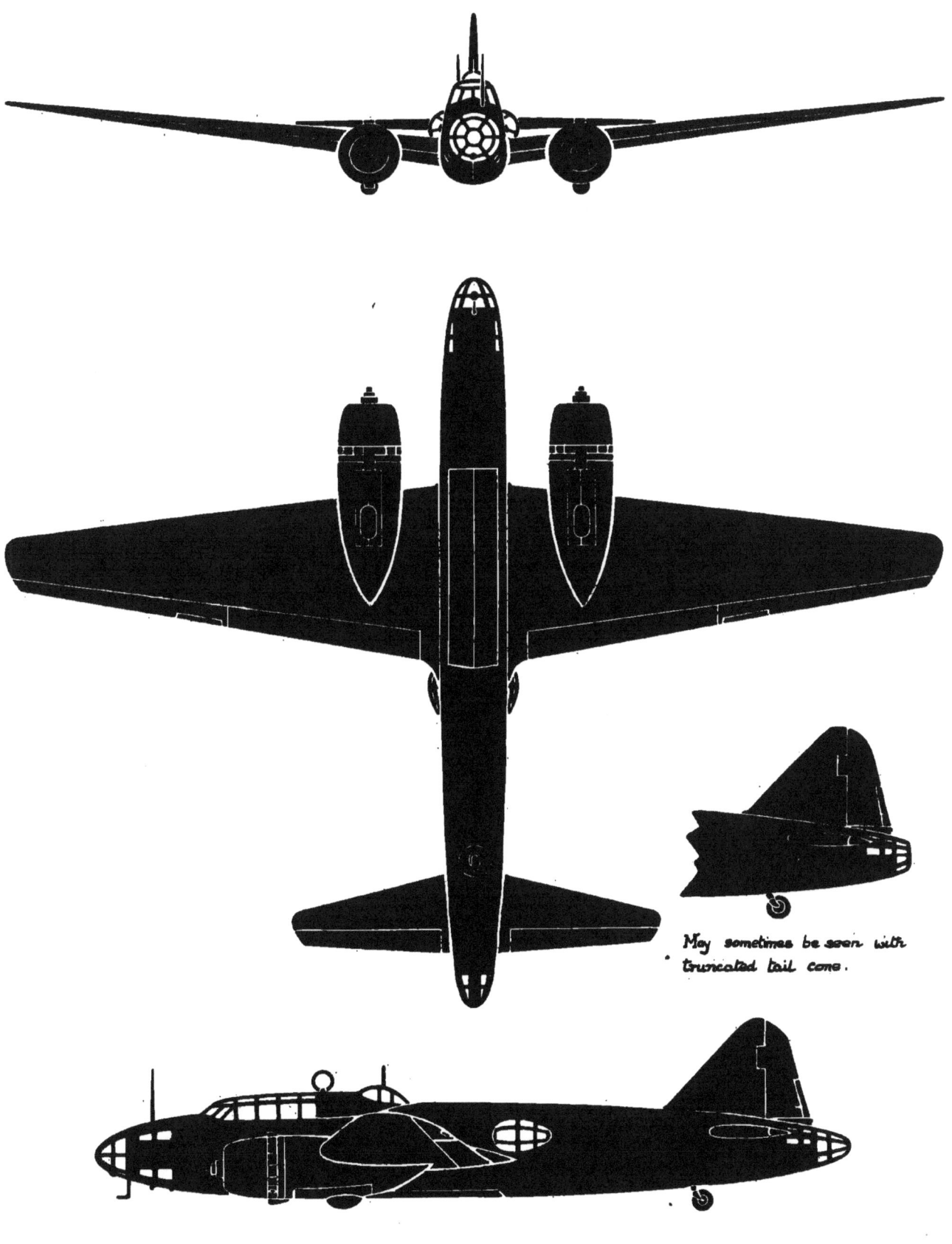

May sometimes be seen with truncated tail cone.

SPAN 82' 4"  **BETTY** BOMBER  LENGTH 65' 6"

Interim Silhouette
A.R. SCHOOL, TRINCOMALEE
Eastern Fleet Issue

Eastern Fleet Chart Production Unit.

SPAN 66' 10"  **FRANCES**  LENGTH 49' 4"
BOMBER

Eastern Fleet Chart Production Unit,

# "FRANCES"

## NAVY. TWIN ENGINED LAND BASED TORPEDO BOMBER

CHARACTERISTICS.

A mid-wing monoplane with dihedral from roots of rather short narrow and equally straight tapered blunt wings.

Two large underslung radial engines in long streamlined cowlings with large spinners.

Short nose, slightly longer than engines, much glazed, running into long slim fuselage unbroken except for short cockpit.

Tall round topped fin/rudder faired into fuselage, large wide spanned diamond shaped tail plane extending to end of fuselage.

CREW.

4.

DIMENSIONS.

Span 66'10". Length 49'4".

SPEED.

Maximum. 310 knots at 20,000 feet. (estimated)
260 knots at sea level.

OPERATIONAL RADIUS.

Maximum for reconnaissance 1,800 miles at 175 knots at 19,000 feet.
Maximum with 800 kg. (1,760 lb) bomb/torpedo—1,050 miles.
Maximum with 250 kg. (550 lb) bombs—1,350 miles.

BOMB LOAD.

Maximum 1 x 800 kg. (1,760 lb) bomb/torpedo internally plus 2 x 550 bombs externally; or 2 x 500 kg. (total 3,300 lb) bombs.

ARMAMENT.

1 x 7.7 mm. machine gun movable in Nose.
1 x 20 mm. cannon at after end of Cockpit.

NOTE.

A new all purpose aircraft of outstanding ability, fast and manœuvrable which first operated in the Marianas in mid 1944. With its crew of four, it is far more economical of manpower than BETTY (whose crew is seven normally and never less than five) and yet carries a similar bomb load and may possibly carry 1 x 21" torpedo. Dive brakes are fitted outboard of engines. For dive bombing, the angle of dive will probably never exceed 60° and will normally be far less.

FRANCES' short nose, short cabin, short wing and round tipped tail surfaces differentiate her from the INVADER (modified BOSTON) with its long nose, enormous engine nacelles behind the long narrow wings and all square extremities and dihedral tail plane.

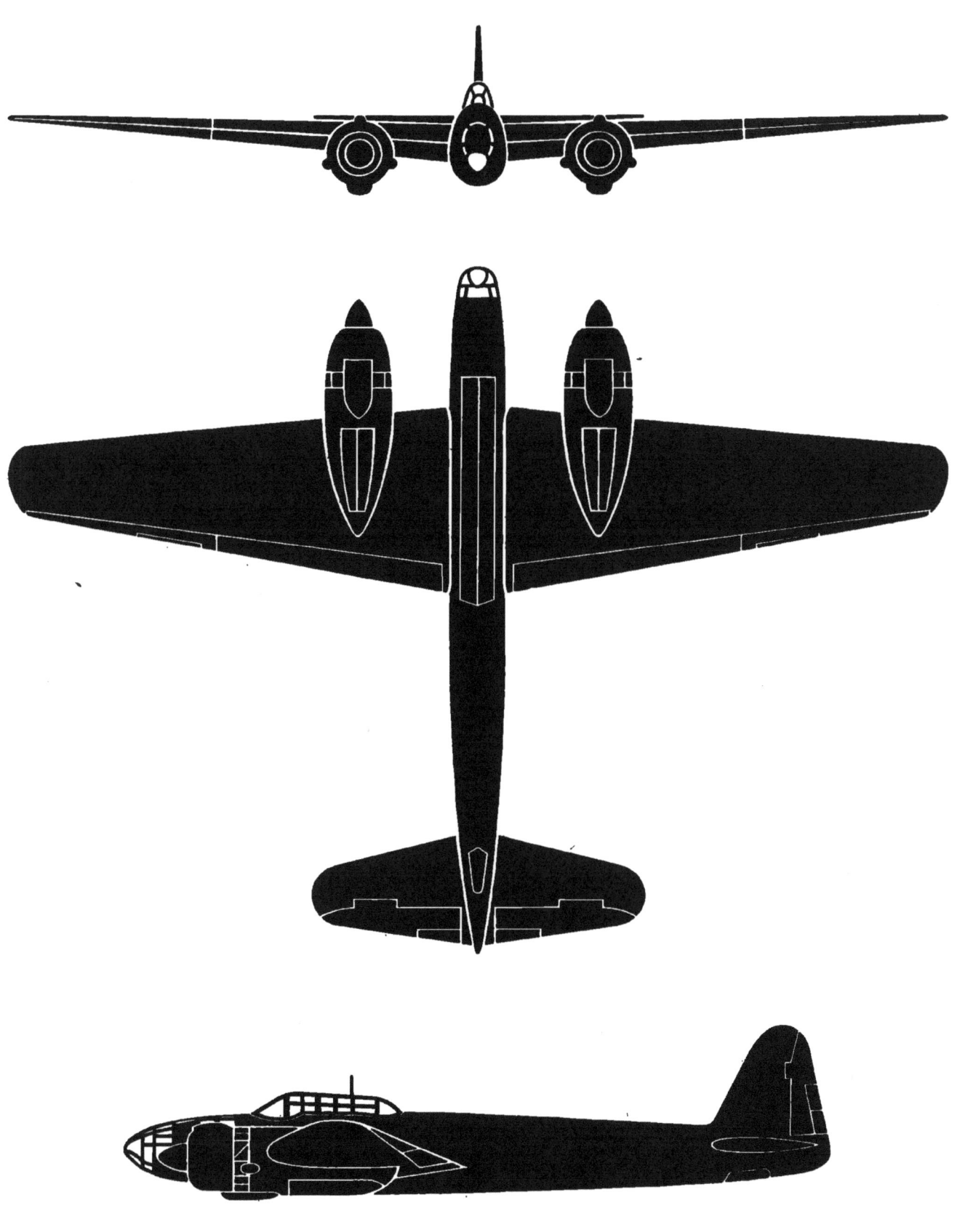

SPAN 66'10"  **FRANCES**  LENGTH 49'4"
BOMBER

Interim Silhouette
A.R. SCHOOL,
TRINCOMALEE.
Eastern Fleet Issue.

Eastern Fleet Chart Production Unit.

SPAN 66' 7" **HELEN** LENGTH 53' 0"
BOMBER

Eastern Fleet Chart Production Unit.

# "HELEN"

## ARMY 100. TWIN ENGINED BOMBER

CHARACTERISTICS.

Mid-wing monoplane with dihedral from roots of broad wings, a wide stepped-forward section between engines adding to apparent width; broad round tips.

Two underslung radial engines in long cowlings.

Deep, long nosed fuselage with raised cabin and slightly curving belly, ending in glazed tail gun position.

Tall raking single fin/rudder with vertical trailing edge; wide back-swept tail plane set high on fuselage.

CREW.

5—7.

DIMENSIONS.

Span 66'7". Length 53'0".

SPEED.

Maximum. 265 knots at 18,000 feet.
230 knots at sea level.

OPERATIONAL RADIUS.

Maximum 1,000 miles (at 170 knots at 18,000 feet) with maximum bombs.
Normal radius 700 miles.

BOMB LOAD.

1 × 500 kg. (1,100 lb) plus 9 × 60 kg. (132 lb) bomb. Total 2,300 lb; or
2 × 500 kg.; or
4 × 250 kg.; or
10 × 100 kg.; or
15 × 50 kg.

ARMAMENT.

1 × 7.7 mm. machine gun in Nose, Lateral (2) and Ventral positions.
1 × 20 mm. cannon in hand operated Dorsal Turret (later turrets are all electric).
1 × 12.7 mm. machine gun in Tail.

NOTE.

At first unsuccessful, HELEN has now become a first line aircraft and will ultimately replace SALLY, so will probably be seen on shipping reconnaissance in this theatre. Improvements in the arc of fire of the tail gun have resulted in the original glazed cone being truncated (c.f., BETTY) the position remaining open except for folding canvas hood.

Large size V wing and tall straight lined tail fin distinguish HELEN from the U winged, Bristol tailed BEAUFORT now obsolescent. HELEN has centred, BEAUFORT underslung engines.

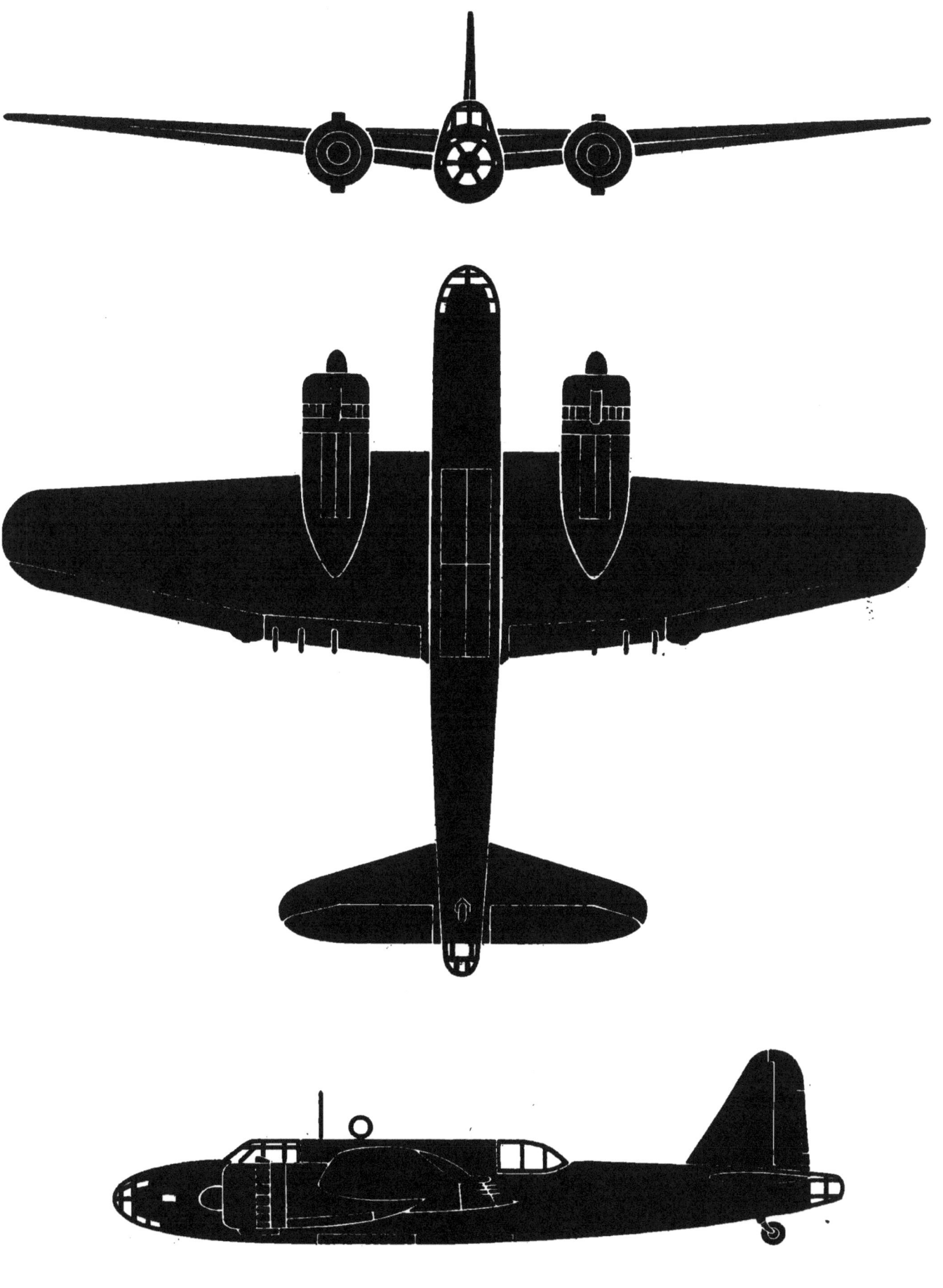

SPAN 48'6"  *JILL*  LENGTH 35'0"
TORPEDO BOMBER

Eastern Fleet Chart Production Unit.

# "JILL"

## NAVY. SINGLE ENGINED CARRIER BORNE TORPEDO BOMBER

CHARACTERISTICS.

Low wing monoplane with dihedral from roots of straight tapered wings, with swept forward pointed tips.

Engine small, compared with wing span, streamlined into short nose.

Fuselage little tapered with long raised glass house.

Tall narrow single fin/rudder, narrow, wide-spanned tailplane set high on the fuselage.

CREW.

2—3.

DIMENSIONS.

Span 48'6". Length 35'0".

SPEED.

Maximum. 285 knots at 17,000 feet.
235 knots at sea level (figure approximate).

OPERATIONAL RADIUS.

Maximum 1,050 miles at 120 knots for reconnaissance.
550 miles with torpedo or full bomb load. (figure estimated)

BOMB LOAD.

1 × 800 kg. (1,760 lb) 18" torpedo or bomb; or
6 × 100 kg. (220 lb) bombs.

ARMAMENT.

1 × 7.7 mm. machine gun in rear of Cockpit.

NOTE.

Replacing KATE, JILL is becoming rapidly the most important single engined torpedo bomber and spreading, as a land based aircraft, to the Indian Ocean area. Speed and operational radius at present uncertain, will probably be a considerable improvement upon KATE, and it is expected that JILL will probably later carry a 21" torpedo. Being equipped with radar, night torpedo attacks should be an important part of JILL's operations.

The small size of JILL's engine, dihedral from roots of low placed wings and round pointed tips to all extremities differentiate it from the AVENGER, with its enormously deep stubby dropbelly fuselage and square cut wings and tail unit.

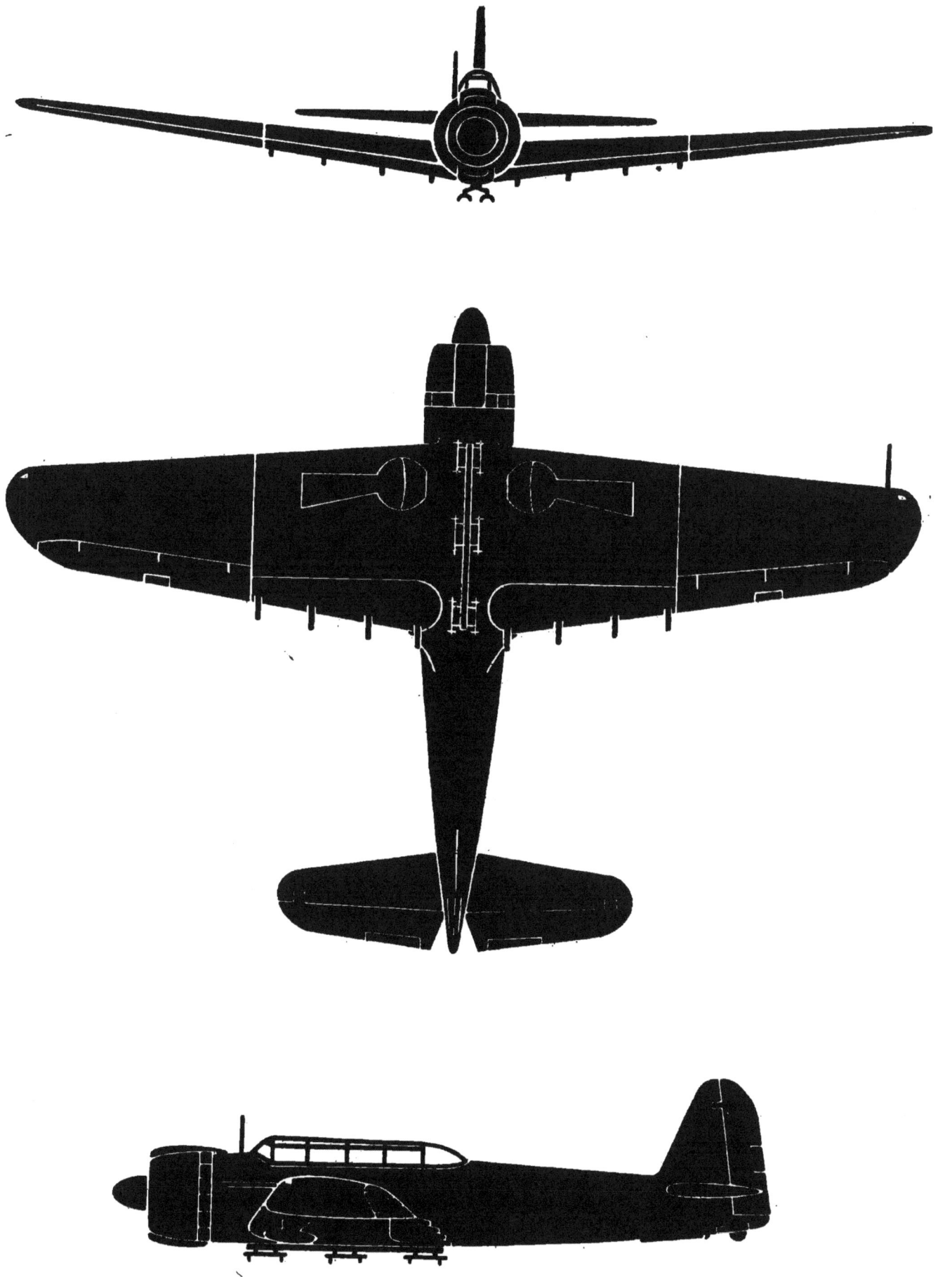

SPAN 48'6"  **JILL**  LENGTH 35'0"
TORPEDO BOMBER

Interim Silhouette
*R. SCHOOL,*
**TRINCOMALEE**
*Eastern Fleet Issue.*

Eastern Fleet Chart Production Unit.

SPAN 37' 9"   **JUDY**   LENGTH 33' 6"
RECONNAISSANCE

# "JUDY"

## NAVY 2. SINGLE IN LINE ENGINED CARRIER BORNE RECONNAISSANCE DIVE BOMBER

CHARACTERISTICS.

Low mid-wing monoplane with short broad straight tapered round tipped wings and dihedral from roots.

In-line engine in downcurved (pointed) nose, prominent radiator just behind propellor.

Long sturdy but tapered fuselage well streamlined, ending in blunt tip.

Low round topped single fin/rudder. Wide-spanned tail plane set high on fuselage.

CREW.
2.

DIMENSIONS.
Span 37'9". Length 33'6".

SPEED.
Maximum. 315 knots at 19,500 feet.
265 knots at sea level.

OPERATIONAL RADIUS.
Maximum for reconnaissance 1,050 miles (extra drop tank carried in place of bomb).

BOMB LOAD.
1 × 250 kg. (530 lb) bomb stowed internally below wings with displacement gear for dive bombing.

ARMAMENT.
2 × 7.7 mm. machine guns over Engine.
1 × 7.7 mm. machine gun in rear of Cockpit.

NOTE.
The only NAVY plane with an in-line engine so far in service. Besides reconnaissance duties it can be and has been used as a dive bomber. No dive brakes are fitted, use being made of flaps when diving. The provision of internal bomb stowage may indicate that JUDY was designed as a successor for VAL, and although now relatively unimportant numerically, in view of its high speed at low levels, it may grow in importance for low level attacks against shipping; and bombing, not reconnaissance, will in future become its primary task.

Unlikely to be confused with any Allied aircraft yet operating.

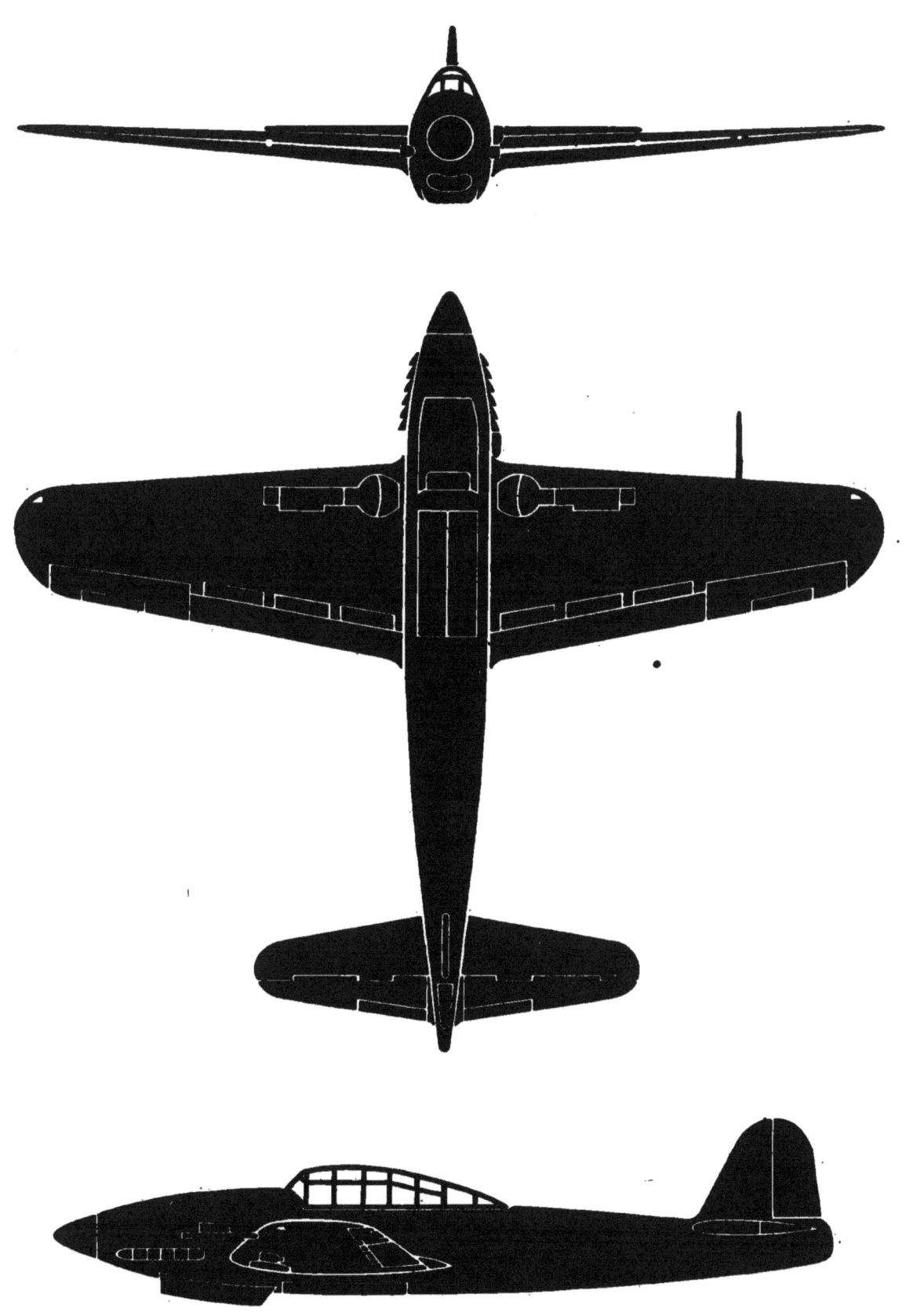

SPAN 37' 9"  **JUDY**  LENGTH 33' 6"
RECONNAISSANCE

Interim Silhouette
A. SCHOOL,
TRINCOMALEE
Eastern Fleet Issue

Eastern Fleet Chart Production Unit.

SPAN 58' 0" **LILY** LENGTH 44' 2"
LIGHT BOMBER

# "LILY"

## ARMY. TWIN ENGINED LIGHT BOMBER AND DIVE BOMBER

CHARACTERISTICS.

A mid wing monoplane with dihedral from roots, straight taper mostly on the leading edge pointed tips.

Two underslung radial engines in short cowlings and with large spinners.

Glazed nose of deep oval section, long raised cabin, flat belly with marked step-up abaft wing roots.

Remainder of fuselage very slim, ending in a point. Tall single fin/rudder, the curved rudder faired into fuselage point. Tailplane large and pointed, tapered on leading edge only.

CREW.

4.

DIMENSIONS.

Span 58'0". Length 44'2".

SPEED.

Maximum.   250 knots at 18,000 feet.
           210 knots at sea level.

OPERATIONAL RADIUS.

Maximum 650 miles as bomber, at 155 knots at 15,500 feet with 440 lb bombs.
550 miles with maximum bombs.

BOMB LOAD.

Maximum 4 × 100 kg. (total 880 lb).

ARMAMENT.

1 × 7.7 mm. machine gun in Nose.
2 × 7.7 mm. machine guns in side of Cabin.
1 × 7.7 mm. machine gun in Belly, firing aft.
1 × 12.7 mm. machine gun in Rear Cockpit or 2 × 7.7 mm. machine guns.

NOTE.

Numerous but not, so far, a very effective machine and apparently unpopular with the Japanese crews, who call it "Flying Coffin." Dive brakes on later models make LILY a potential threat to shipping during an amphibious operation. Some models may have a 12.7 mm. machine gun, hand operated, in the rear of the glass-house, reducing its apparent length. This change to a 12.7 mm. machine-gun is the first of a series of developments which may improve LILY's performance as a fighting machine. It is also possible that amongst armament changes will be a fixed tail gun, perhaps 12.7 mm., remotely controlled .

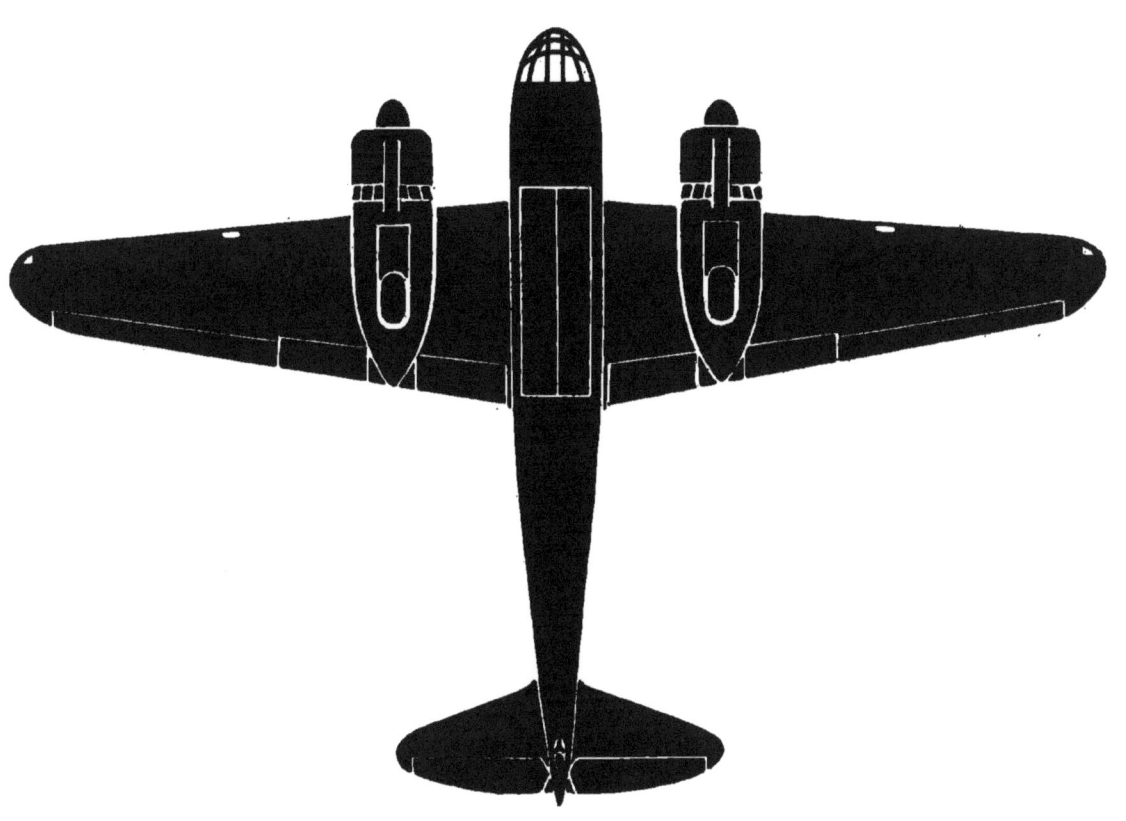

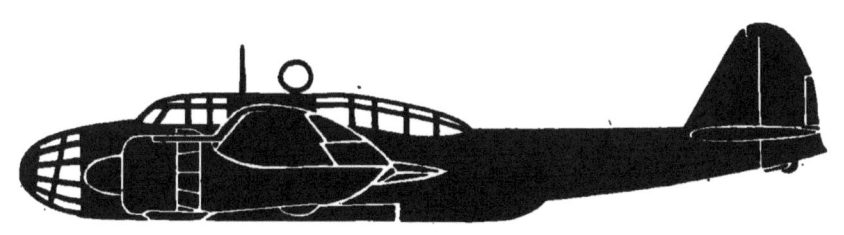

SPAN 58' 0"  **LILY**  LENGTH 44' 2"
LIGHT BOMBER

Eastern Fleet Chart Production Unit.

*Interim Silhouette*
**Æ. SCHOOL,
TRINCOMALEE**
*Eastern Fleet Issue*

# "LIZ"

## NAVY 2. FOUR ENGINED LAND BASED BOMBER

CHARACTERISTICS.

Mid-wing monoplane with dihedral from roots of long-pointed swept-back wings, only slight taper being on the trailing edge.

Four centred radial engines set relatively closely together.

Deep little-glazed nose ending in conical gun position. Flat belly to after wing root, where marked step-up allows for gun position. Back straight with centrally-placed turret.

Wide, almost rectangular tail plane, leading edge only tapered slightly, set on hump above fuselage line; twin oval (?) fins and rudders at end of tail plane.

CREW.

7—8. (?)

DIMENSIONS.

Span 138'3". Length 101'9".

SPEED.

Maximum 275 knots at 20,00 feet.
230 knots at sea level.

OPERATIONAL RADIUS.

Maximum 1,400 miles for reconnaissance only.

BOMB LOAD.

Possibly 3 × 800 kg (1,760 lb) torpedoes (total 5,280 lb) with maximum bomb stowage of 6—7,000 lb. One torpedo internally and one under each wing.

ARMAMENT.

Provision for probably six gun positions—most of which could be 20 mm. cannons.

NOTE.

With the advent of engines of the 2,000 h.p. class, LIZ has become operational in small numbers in the S.W. Pacific. Previously little had been seen of this aircraft although its existence as a transport was known, and its lack of success was mainly due to its being underpowered. Carrying three torpedoes and equipped for night flying, LIZ constitutes a threat to shipping over a wide area.

The marked sweep back and straight trailing edge; the dropped belly-line of a long fuselage and small twin fins, are great points of difference between LIZ and the LIBERATOR, which has very long slim wings, short stumpy fuselage and enormous twin fins.

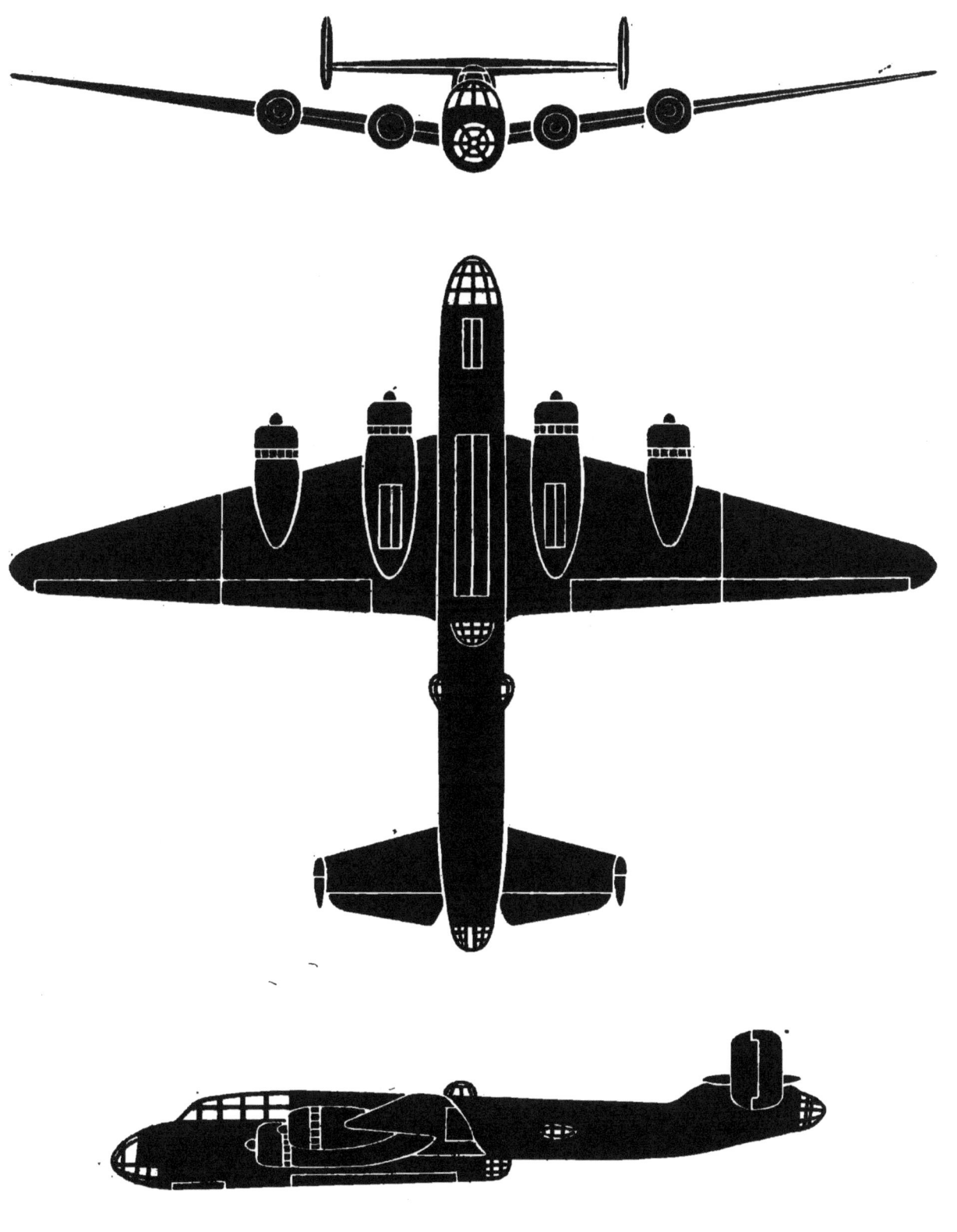

SPAN 110' 0"  **LIZ**  LENGTH 80' 0"
BOMBER

Eastern Fleet Chart Production Unit.

*Interim Silhouette*
**A.R. SCHOOL,
TRINCOMALEE**
*Eastern Fleet Issue.*

SPAN 50' 11"  **KATE**  LENGTH 33' 11"

TORPEDO BOMBER

Eastern Fleet Chart Production Unit.

# "KATE"

## NAVY 97. SINGLE ENGINED CARRIER BORNE TORPEDO BOMBER

CHARACTERISTICS.

A low wing monoplane with sharp dihedral from a narrow flat centre section. Wings long and tapering with pointed tips.

Small radial engine in relatively long slim nose.

Fuselage slim and exceptionally short between wing and tailplane.

Tall, narrow round-topped fin/rudder. Small but broad diamond-shaped tail plane set at end of fuselage.

CREW.

2—3, usually 2.

DIMENSIONS.

Span 50′11″. Length 33′11″.

SPEED.

Maximum 195 knots at 8,500 feet.
170 knots at sea level.

OPERATIONAL RADIUS.

Maximum 650 miles.
530 miles normally.

BOMB LOAD.

1 × 800 kg. torpedo or bomb 1,760 lb, or
2 × 250 kg. (530 lb) bombs, or
6 × 60 kg. (132 lb) bombs.

ARMAMENT.

1 × 7.7 mm. machine gun in rear cockpit.

NOTE.

An old, but still useful and prevalent torpedo bomber, responsible for most of the damage at Pearl Harbour. Prominent feature in flight is the externally slung torpedo carried at a considerable angle from the horizontal. Now being rapidly replaced in the Indian Ocean by JILL, but still operational there and in the Pacific. Used for night torpedo attack, illuminating its targets by flares, but Radar recently fitted. KATE has on occasion carried a heavier, 21″, torpedo.

KATE's pointed wing tips and slim fuselage behind small engine distinguish her from the mid-winged tubby AVENGER, which has square cut wings and tail fin/rudder. The marked reversed curve of fuselage behind wings of DAUNTLESS, with its short broad round wings and triangular tail fin/rudder makes confusion difficult.

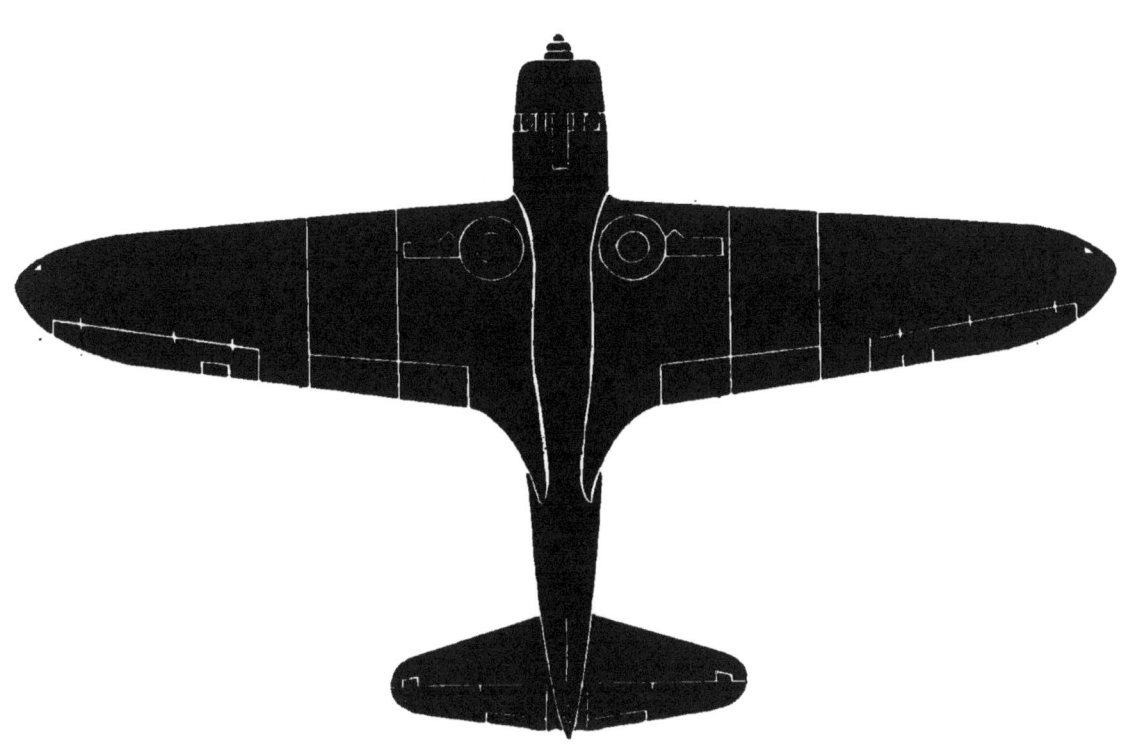

SPAN 50' 11"  **KATE**  LENGTH 33' 11"
TORPEDO BOMBER

Interim Silhouette
**A.R. SCHOOL,
TRINCOMALEE**
Eastern Fleet Issue.

Eastern Fleet Chart Production Unit.

SPAN 82' 0"  **NELL**  LENGTH 52' 6"
BOMBER

# "NELL"

## NAVY 96. TWIN ENGINED BOMBER AND TORPEDO BOMBER

CHARACTERISTICS.

Mid-wing monoplane with long straight tapered wings, broad at roots and narrow at square tips. Junkers flaps are fitted.

Two small underslung radial engines set close into nose.

Fuselage slim and very short with solid nose. Side blisters and two dorsal "turrets" may be carried but are not constant.

Wide square-tipped tail plane, twin angular fins and rudders set wholly above tail plane at half span.

CREW.

7.

DIMENSIONS.

Span 82'0". Length 54'0".

SPEED.

Maximum 195 knots at 21,000 feet.
175 knots at sea level.

OPERATIONAL RADIUS.

Maximum for reconnaissance 1,350 miles.
750 miles with full bomb load.

BOMB LOAD.

Maximum 2,200 lb.
Normal, 1,540 lb (2 × 250 kg., plus 4 × 50 kg. bombs), or
1 × 18" 800 kg. (1,760 lb) torpedo carried externally.

ARMAMENT.

1 × 7.7 mm. machine gun fixed in solid Nose.
2 × 7.7 mm. machine guns from forward Cabin.
2 × 7.7 mm. machine guns in Lateral Blisters.
1 × 20 mm. cannon  } from Dorsal "Turrets."
1 × 7.7 mm. machine gun
1 × 7.7 mm. machine gun Ventrally.

NOTE.

An old machine, responsible for the sinkings of the *Prince of Wales* and *Repulse*. Modifications, however, make the latest NELL still a useful aircraft, sightings of which are not as rare as might be expected from her age—most are, however, operating from S.W. and Central Pacific bases.

Variations in armament are common and the one above is probably a maximum.
Unlike any Allied aircraft operating in this Theatre

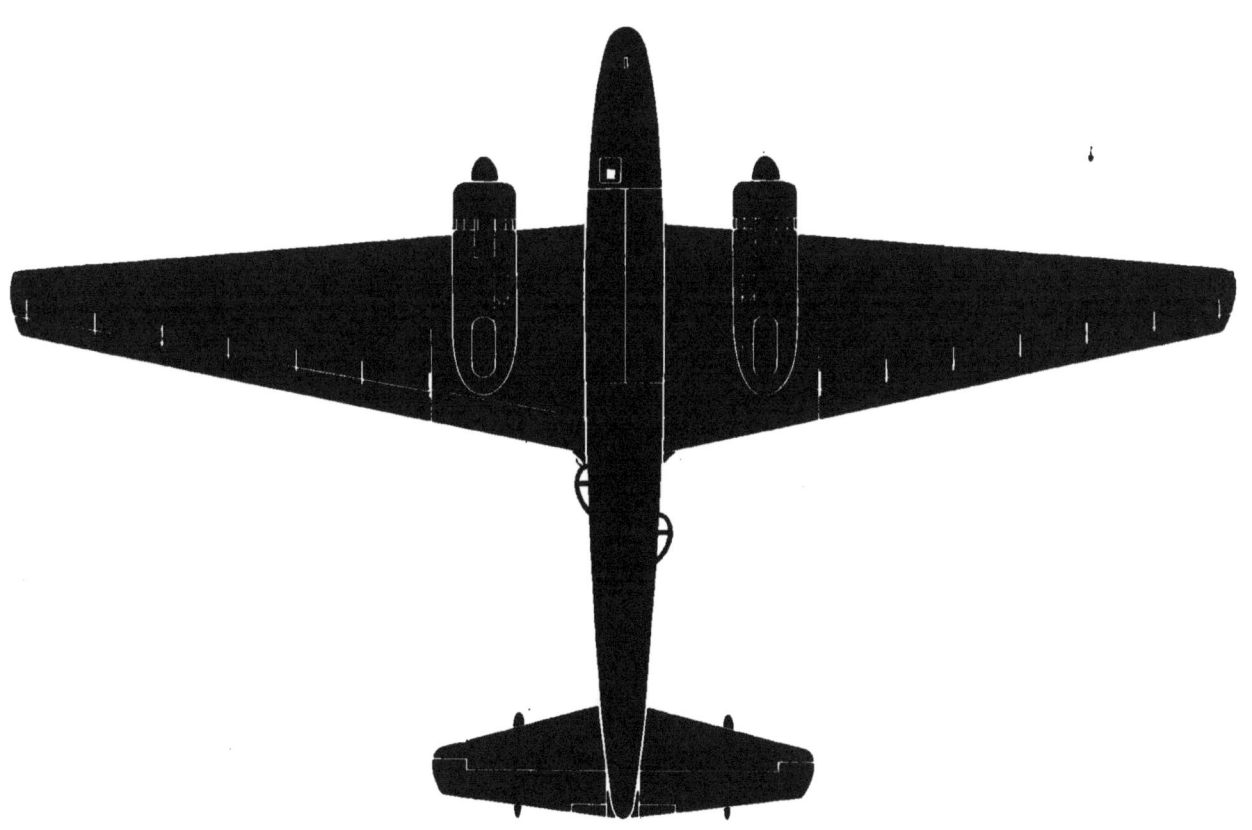

SPAN 82' 0"     **NELL**     LENGTH 52' 6"
BOMBER

*Interim Silhouette*
*A.R. SCHOOL,*
*TRINCOMALEE*
*Eastern Fleet Issue*

Eastern Fleet Chart Production Unit.

SPAN 74' 8"  **SALLY**  LENGTH 52' 0"
BOMBER

Eastern Fleet Chart Production Unit.

# "SALLY"

## ARMY 97. TWIN ENGINED BOMBER

CHARACTERISTICS.

Mid-wing monoplane with broad equally straight tapered wings, with dihedral almost from roots.

Two underslung radial engines in short cowlings.

Short glazed nose, short fuselage compared with wing span, ending in blunt tail cone behind tail unit.

Tall upright fin/rudder, large wide triangular tail plane.

CREW.

7.

DIMENSIONS.

Span 74'8". Length 52'0".

SPEED.

Maximum. 250 knots at 15,000 feet.
215 knots at sea level.

OPERATIONAL RADIUS.

Maximum 920 miles (at 140 knots at 15,000 feet).
800 miles (at 140 knots at 15,000 feet) with 500 kg. (1,100 lb) bomb.

BOMB LOAD.

16 × 50 kg. (110 lb) bombs, total 1,760 lb, or
9 × 100 kg. (220 lb) bombs, total 1,980 lb, or
4 × 250 kg. (550 lb) bombs, total 2,200 lb, or
2 × 500 kg. (1,100 lb) bombs, total 2,200 lb.
Normal load 12 × 50 kg. bomb.

ARMAMENT.

1 × 7.7 mm. machine gun in Nose, each Beam position, Tail Cone (remote control) and Ventral position. (5 × 7.7 mm. machine guns in all.)
1 × 12.7 mm. machine gun in hand operated Turret just behind trailing edge of wing.

NOTE.

Important as a shipping reconnaissance aircraft, SALLY is being kept operational, despite age, because of the original drawbacks found with BETTY and HELEN. Still the backbone of the Army bombers it is, however, being replaced by the now improved HELEN, both against shore and shipping targets, mostly in the Bay of Bengal. SALLY's petrol tanks are poorly protected so she is vulnerable against small arms fire.

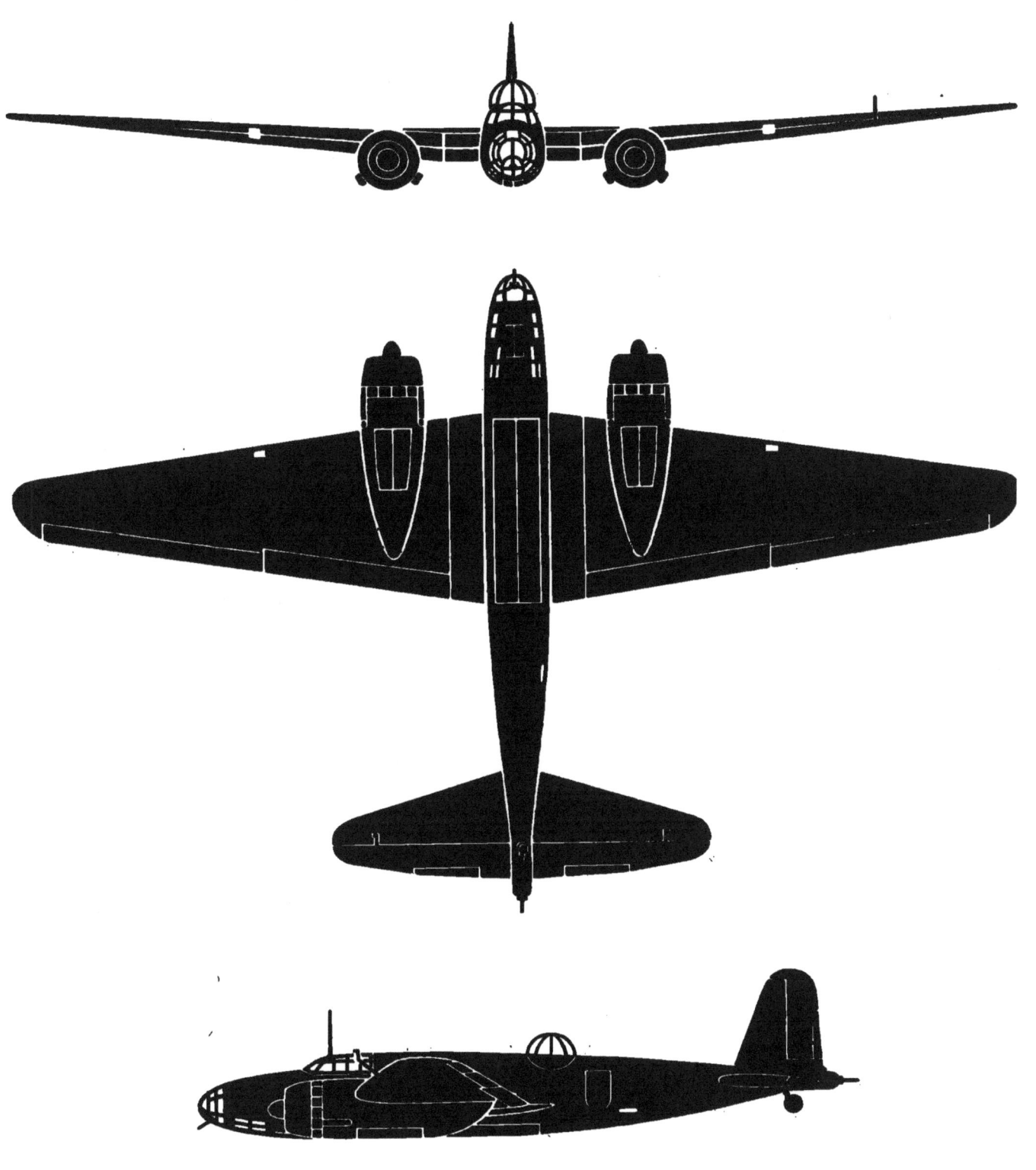

SPAN 47' 7"  **VAL**  LENGTH 35' 5"
DIVE BOMBER

Eastern Fleet Chart Production Unit

# "VAL"

## NAVY 99. SINGLE ENGINED CARRIER BORNE DIVE BOMBER

**CHARACTERISTICS.**

Low-wing monoplane, with dihedral from flat centre section of elliptical wing. Fixed spatted undercarriage at ends of centre section. Dive brakes outside undercarriage.

Single, relatively small radial engine in short cowling.

Fuselage slim, ending in point abaft tail unit. Short glazed cockpit.

Large fin reaches almost to cockpit, sweeping up to pointed tip of rudder. Tail plane small and tapered on leading edge.

**CREW.**

2.

**DIMENSIONS.**

Span 47'7". Length 35'5".

**SPEED.**

Maximum 215 knots at 21,000 feet.
190 knots at sea level.

**OPERATIONAL RADIUS.**

Maximum 650 miles at 105 knots with $2 \times 100$ kg. bombs.
500 miles at 105 knots with maximum bombs.

**BOMB LOAD.**

Maximum $1 \times 250$ kg. (550 lb) bomb centrally.
$2 \times 100$ kg. (220 lb) bombs on wing racks outside dive brakes.
Total weight 990 lb.
Central bomb replaceable by drop petrol tank.

**ARMAMENT.**

$2 \times 7.7$ mm. machine guns over Engine.
$1 \times 7.7$ mm. machine gun in after end of Cockpit.

**NOTE.**

Numerically relatively unimportant. Still operational in S.W. and C. Pacific, mostly land based. Developed as counterpart of JU 87, VAL is strongly built since lightness is not necessary in an aircraft designed to act as dive bomber. The original VAL had a straight tapered leading edge and round wing tips, but is now obsolete. A recent addition to VAL's armament takes the form of rocket projectiles (? up to eight may be carried ?).

SPAN 47' 7"  **VAL**  LENGTH 35' 5"
DIVE BOMBER

Eastern Fleet Chart Production Unit.

*Interim Silhouette*
**AR. SCHOOL, TRINCOMALEE**
*Eastern Fleet Issue*

# RECONNAISSANCE

SPAN 48' 6"  **DINAH**  LENGTH 36' 1"
RECONNAISSANCE

# "DINAH"

## ARMY 100. TWIN ENGINED RECONNAISSANCE PLANE

CHARACTERISTICS.

Low-wing monoplane with considerable dihedral from roots of straight tapered blunt tipped wings.

Two centred radial engines, in short streamlined cowlings, with large spinners.

Short pointed nose, just longer than engine, raised cabin flowing into fuselage aft, giving good streamlined appearance.

Low sloping fin and nearly vertical and blunt tipped rudder. Narrow tapered tail plane.

CREW.

2.

DIMENSIONS.

Span 48'6". Length 36'1".

SPEED.

Maximum.   340 knots at 21,500 feet.
           275 knots at sea level.

OPERATIONAL RADIUS.

Maximum 720 miles (at 180 knots at 21,500 feet).

BOMB LOAD.

None carried.

ARMAMENT.

Normally none carried, sometimes 1 × 7.7 mm. machine gun in rear of Cockpit and 1 × 50 mm. mortar bomb thrower, throwing $2\frac{1}{4}$ lb bombs.

NOTE.

Used by both Army and Navy, DINAH has been given the name of "H.Q. RECONNAISSANCE PLANE." Normally not very important to the Fleet as an offensive aircraft. Allied Fighters approaching from astern at same altitude have, however, been dealt with severely by means of the mortar bomb thrower, which can project these missiles to about 200—400 yard ranges.

Compare with NICK and IRVING.

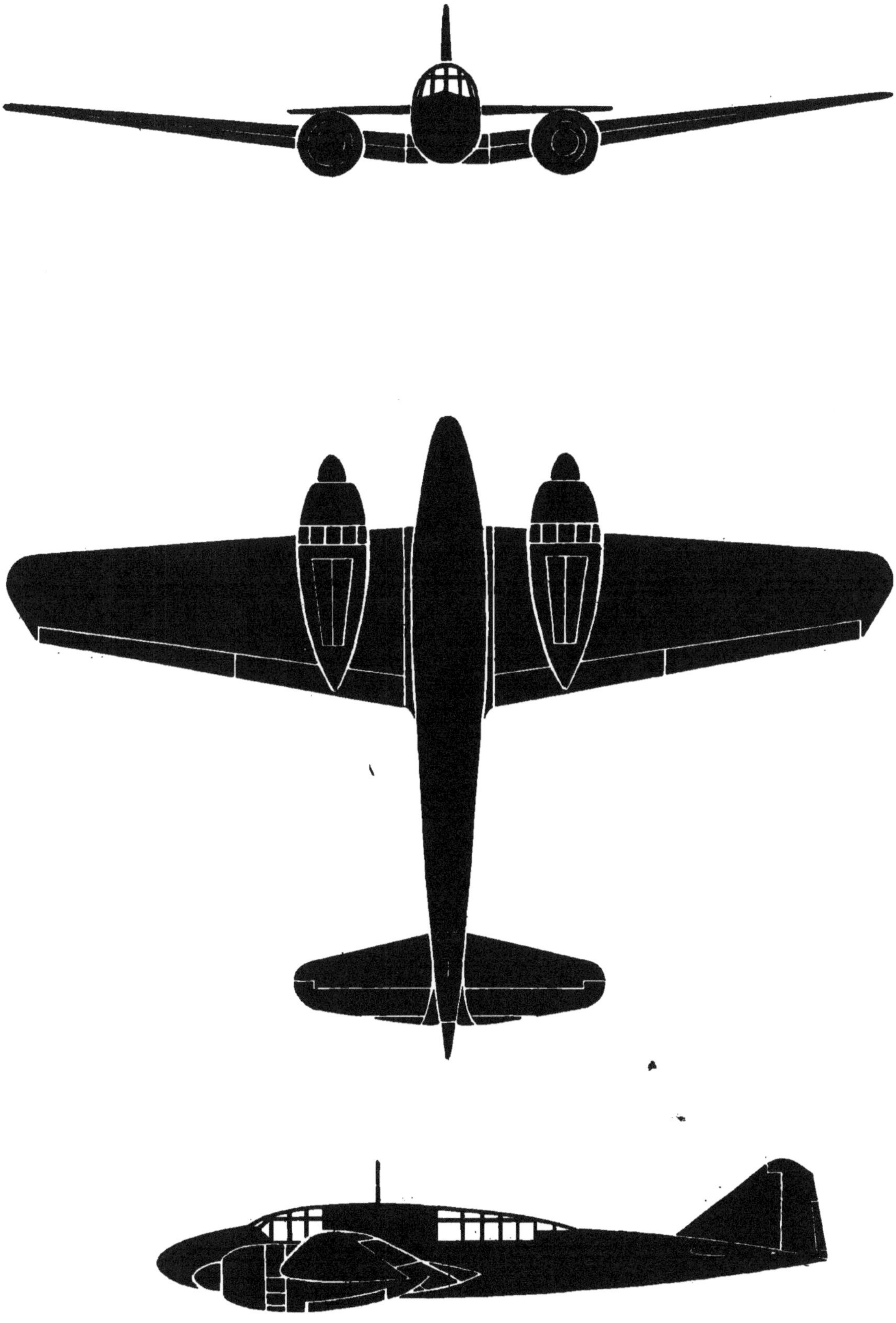

SPAN 48' 6"  **DINAH**  LENGTH 36' 1"
RECONNAISSANCE

Eastern Fleet Chart Production Unit.

*Interim Silhouette*
**A.R. SCHOOL,
TRINCOMALEE**
*Eastern Fleet Issue.*

SPAN 124' 0"  **EMILY**  LENGTH 96' 6"
RECONNAISSANCE

# "EMILY"

## NAVY 2. FOUR ENGINED FLYING BOAT

**CHARACTERISTICS.**

Large high wing flying boat with straight tapered long wings and narrow round tips. Stabilising floats set well in from wing tips.

Four centred radial engines, small in relation to wing thickness.

Long deep hull with gently curving nose. Turrets in nose, tail and in back behind wings.

Broad squat round tipped fin/rudder, relatively small round tipped tail plane.

**CREW.**

8—10.

**DIMENSIONS.**

Span 124'6". Length 92'5".

**SPEED.**

Maximum. 255 knots at 13,000 feet (normal "shadowing" height).
215 knots at sea level.

**OPERATIONAL RADIUS.**

Maximum for reconnaissance 2,100 miles at 120 knots at 1,500 feet.
1,900 miles with 1,000 kg. (2,200 lb) bombs.

**BOMB LOAD.**

2 × 800 kg. (1,760 lb) bombs or torpedoes or up to 16 × 60 kg. (130 lb) bombs—carried in racks under wings between engines.

**ARMAMENT.**

Nose, Tail and Dorsal turrets and two Waist guns are 20 mm. cannon.
4 × 7.7 mm. machine guns also carried as auxiliary armament.

**NOTE.**

A very efficient and fast flying boat which is rapidly replacing the older MAVIS in this theatre. Used extensively on armed reconnaissance, its long endurance (28 hours at 160 knots maximum, or more normally 20 hours) makes it ideal for shadowing. In this area, based on the Andaman Islands, it covered the Bay of Bengal and the Indian Ocean. Despite its formidable armament, it is apparently vulnerable to Fighter attack from below and some armament is likely (?) to appear housed in the belly of the hull, behind after step.

Although just "gull winged," this feature is not noticeable in flight except from dead ahead and should not be stressed as a recognition feature.

EMILY's long nose and long straight tapered round tipped wings distinguish her from the dumpier hulled and short pointed winged SUNDERLAND.

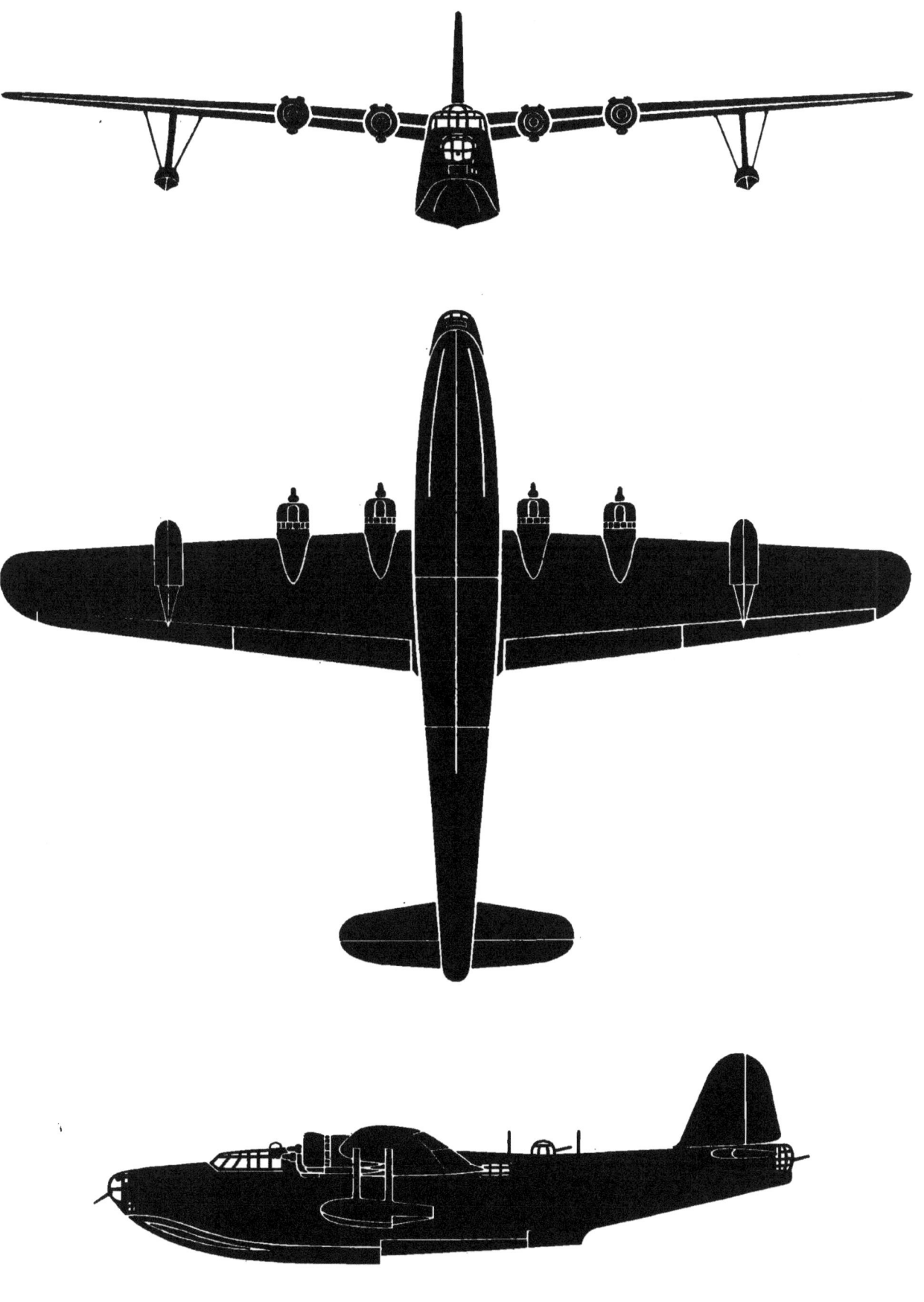

SPAN 124' 0"   **EMILY**   LENGTH 96' 6"
RECONNAISSANCE

Interim Silhouette
AR. SCHOOL,
TRINCOMALEE.
Eastern Fleet Issue.

SPAN 47'6"  **JAKE**  LENGTH 36'11"
RECONNAISSANCE

Eastern Fleet Chart Production Unit.

# "JAKE"

## NAVY 0.  SINGLE ENGINED TWIN FLOAT RECONNAISSANCE PLANE

CHARACTERISTICS.

A low wing monoplane with wide flat centre section, straight leading edge to broad round-pointed tips. Trailing edge curve-tapered giving appearance of elliptical wing. Two long floats strutted to wings, project ahead of nose.

Small radial engine with large spinner—slim nose.

Fuselage with long raised glasshouse and up-curved belly.

Large curve tapered tail plane set well aft of tall round topped fin/rudder.

CREW.

2—3.

DIMENSIONS.

Span 47'6". Length 36'11" (overall).

SPEED.

Maximum.  210 knots at 7,500 feet.
170 knots at sea level.

OPERATIONAL RADIUS.

Maximum.  600 miles approx.

BOMB LOAD.

4 × 60 kg. (132 lb) bombs or
2 × 100 kg. (220 lb) bombs. } often A/S bombs.

ARMAMENT.

1 × 7.7 mm. machine gun in rear of Cockpit.
1 × 20 mm. cannon in Nose ? (unconfirmed position).

NOTE.

Carried by both battleships and cruisers, JAKE is more commonly used in all areas as shore based anti-submarine reconnaissance and patrol aircraft. Often used in S.W. Pacific at dawn or dusk with engine cut to attack M.T.B.s and submarines with bombs and cannon fire from a low level. May become more important as A/S plane and be backed up by new types thought already to be in production ("PAUL"; see last section on New Aircraft).

Twin floats and very flat wing distinguish JAKE from KINGFISHER which has single large central float and sharp dihedral on very broad wing, and two small wing-tip stabilising floats.

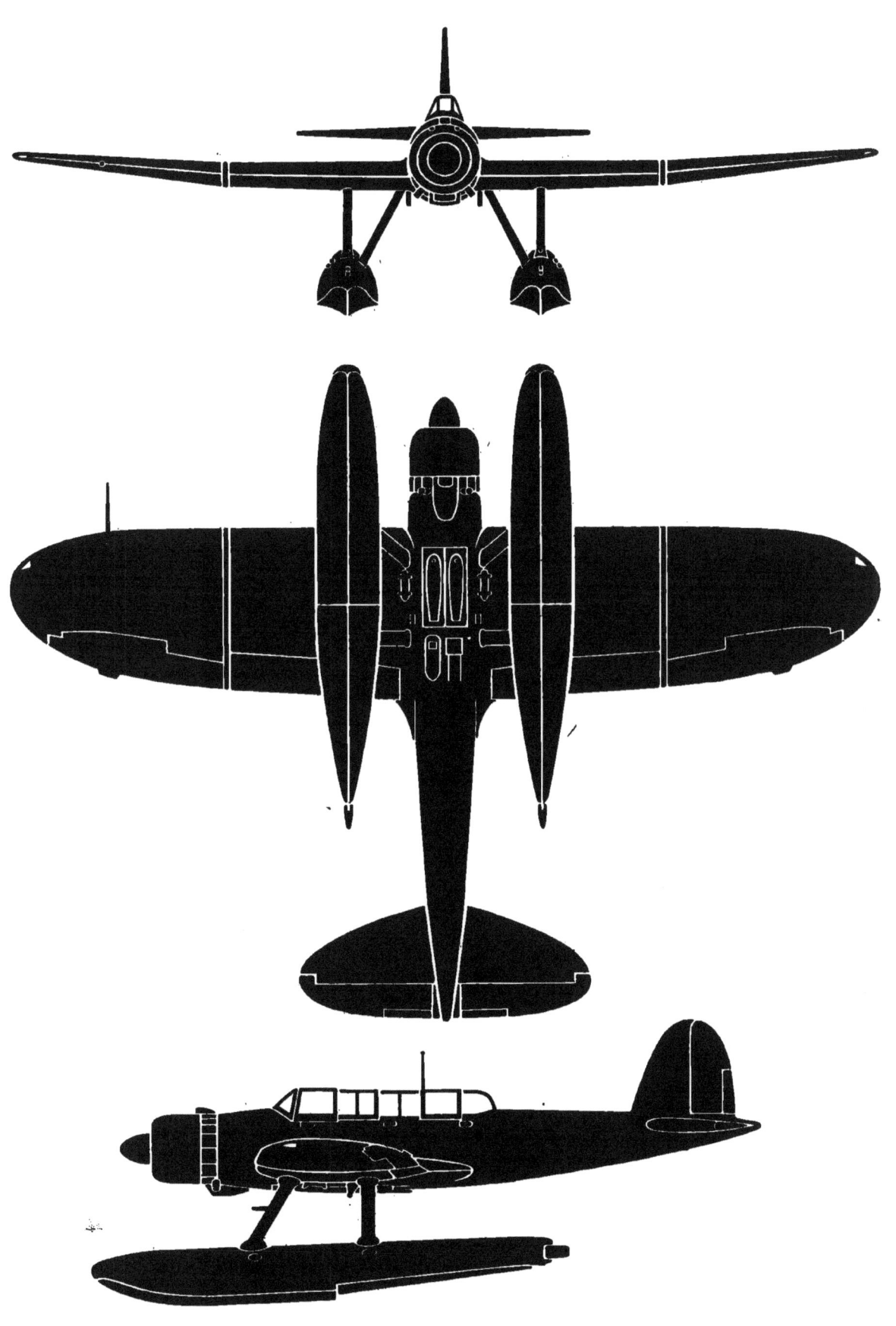

SPAN 47'6"  **JAKE**  LENGTH 36'11"
RECONNAISSANCE

*Interim Silhouette*
**A.R. SCHOOL,
TRINCOMALEE.**
*Eastern Fleet Issue.*

SPAN 36'  **PETE**  LENGTH 31'4"
RECONNAISSANCE

# "PETE"

## NAVY 0. SINGLE ENGINED RECONNAISSANCE BIPLANE

CHARACTERISTICS.

Wings of practically equal span. Upper wing strutted above fuselage and set forward of lower wing. Broken taper on both give appearance of elliptical wings. Small wing tip floats.

Radial engine in short cowling.

Tubby, well streamlined fuselage with two partially glazed cockpits. Large central float attached by thick leg.

Tall large single fin/rudder and elliptical tail plane set forward of rudder.

CREW.

2.

DIMENSIONS.

Span 36'0". Length 31'4".

SPEED.

Maximum. 190 knots at 14,000 feet.
160 knots at sea level.

OPERATIONAL RADIUS.

Maximum. 360 miles (at 115 knots at 14,000 feet).

BOMB LOAD.

2 × 60 kg. (132 lb) anti-submarine or G.P. bombs.

ARMAMENT.

2 × 7.7 mm. machine guns over Engine.
1 × 7.7 mm. machine gun in rear Cockpit.

NOTE.

Although the principal catapult aircraft in use on major units of the Japanese Fleet, PETE is better known as a coastal reconnaissance and anti-submarine and M.G.B. aircraft—most attacks being at dawn or dusk in S.W. and C. Pacific. Otherwise PETE is not particularly important as an offensive aircraft.

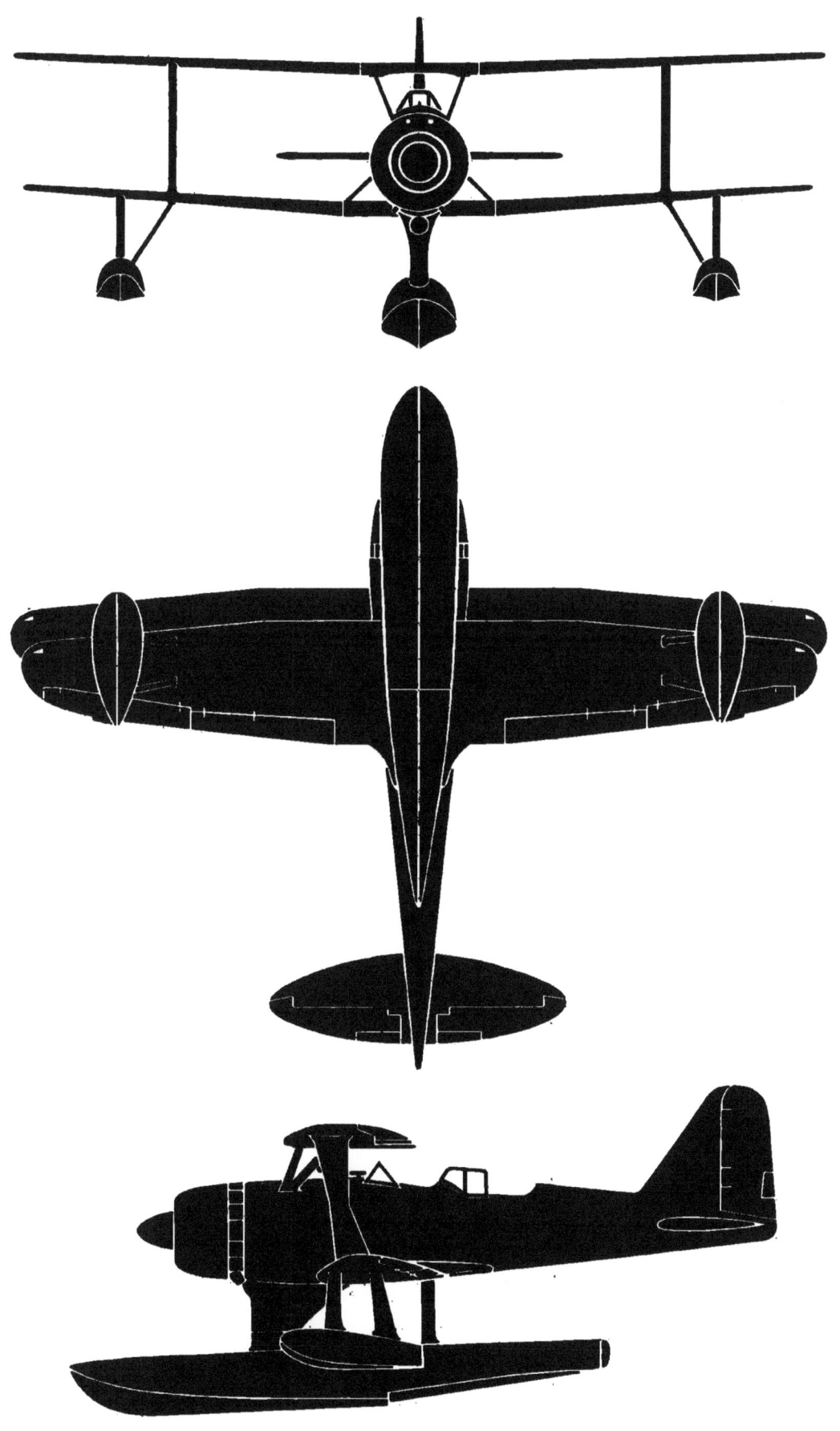

SPAN 36' **PETE** LENGTH 31'4"
RECONNAISSANCE
*Interim Silhouette*
**ÆR. SCHOOL, TRINCOMALEE**
*Eastern Fleet Issue*

Eastern Fleet Chart Production Unit.

SPAN 130' 0"   **MAVIS**   LENGTH 84' 6"
FLYING BOAT

## "MAVIS"

### NAVY 97. FOUR ENGINED PARASOL WINGED FLYING BOAT

CHARACTERISTICS.

Parasol winged monoplane of large size, with long narrow wings tapered from wide rectangular centre section to blunt round tips and strongly strutted to hull. Stabilising floats set at half span and strutted to hull and wings.

Four small radial engines set close together in middle third of wing.

Long slender shallow hull, with rear portion sweeping up to tail turret. Nose and dorsal turrets and lateral blisters commonly fitted.

Wide tail plane set high, twin angular fins/rudders at half span wholly above tail plane.

CREW.

8—10.

DIMENSIONS.

Span 131'0". Length 82'0".

SPEED.

Maximum. 185 knots at 13,500 feet.
160 knots at sea level.

OPERATIONAL RADIUS.

Maximum. 1,130 miles reconnaissance only, at 100 knots at 13,500 feet.
1,000 miles with normal bombs.
7/900 miles with maximum bombs.

BOMB LOAD.

Maximum. 2 × 800 kg. (1,760 lb) torpedoes (possible).
Normal. 4 × 100 kg. (220 lb) bombs.

ARMAMENT.

1 × 7.7 mm. machine gun in Nose Turret and Lateral Blisters.
1 × 20 mm. cannon in Dorsal and Tail Turrets.

NOTE.

Relatively few in service, having been replaced by the much faster and more heavily armed EMILY. Until recently stationed at the Andaman Islands, most have been withdrawn to Central and S.W. Pacific.

Unlike any Allied aircraft in operation.

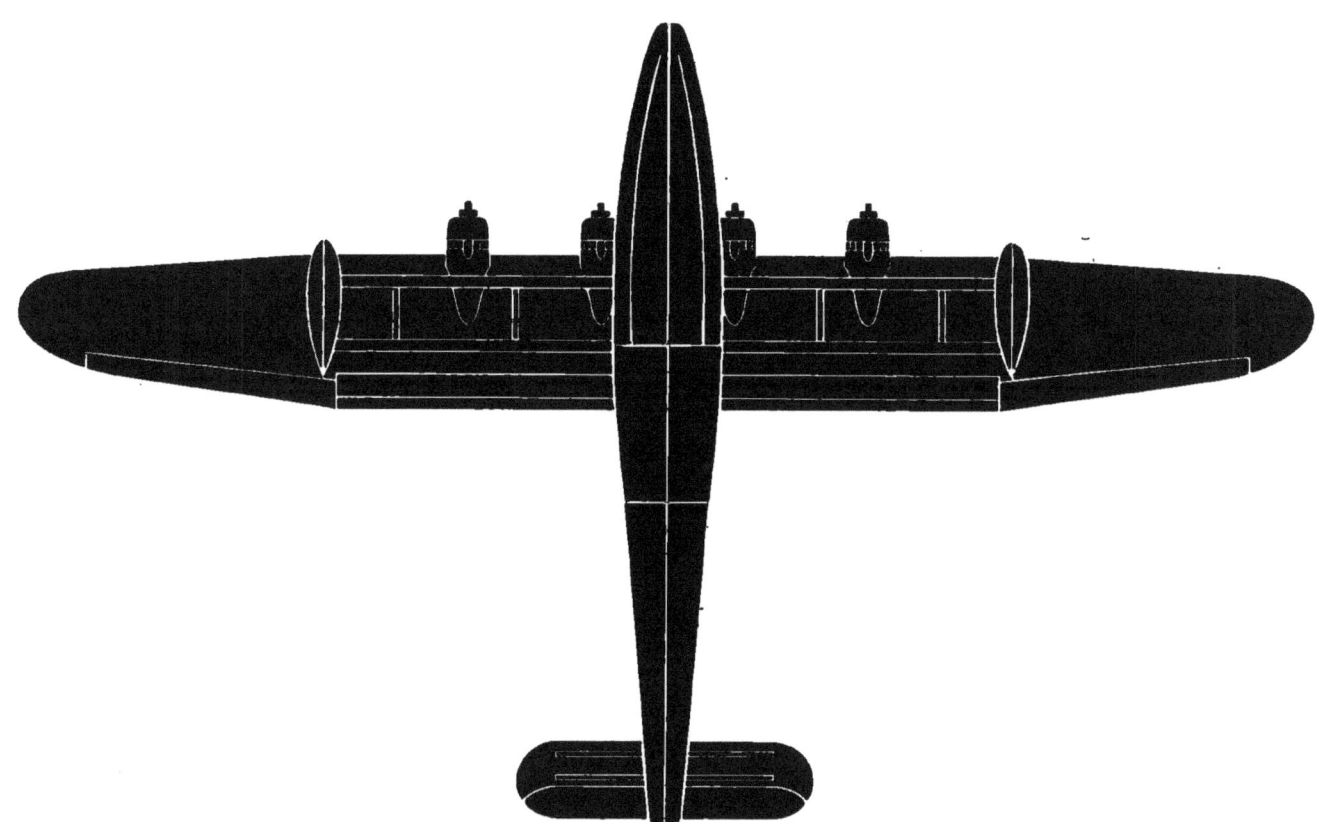

SPAN 130' 0" **MAVIS** LENGTH 84' 6"
FLYING BOAT

Eastern Fleet Chart Production Unit,

Interim Silhouette
AR. SCHOOL,
TRINCOMALEE
Eastern Fleet Issue

SPAN 55' 0"   *IRVING*   LENGTH 38' 6"
RECONNAISSANCE FIGHTER

# "IRVING"

## NAVY 2. TWIN ENGINED LAND BASED RECONNAISSANCE FIGHTER

CHARACTERISTICS.

Low wing monoplane with dihedral from roots of narrow tapering wings—most taper being on the trailing edge—and pointed swept-forward tips.

Two large partly underslung engines in long cowlings.

Short pointed nose only slightly longer than engines, deep narrow fuselage with stepped down cabin top aft.

Large single fin and curved rudder—wide tailplane set at end of fuselage.

CREW.

2—3.

DIMENSIONS.

Span 55'0". Length 38'6".

SPEED.

Maximum. 300 knots at 19,000 feet (estimated).
240 knots at sea level.

OPERATIONAL RADIUS.

Maximum. 750 miles (at 180 knots at 13,000 feet).
Can carry long range auxiliary tanks under wings outside engines so radius may increase in reconnaissance version.

BOMB LOAD.

2 × 60 kg. (132 lb) air burst bombs at wing roots.
3 × 250 kg. (550 lb) bombs slung externally below fuselage.

ARMAMENT.

Not yet crystallised but probably:—

1 × 20 mm. or larger and
2 × 7.7 mm. machine guns } fixed in solid Nose, plus

2 × twin 7.7 mm. machine guns in turrets in rear Cockpit, or

2 × 20 mm. dorsal and
2 × 20 mm. ventral cannons } firing obliquely forward from after Cockpit and used in night fighting.

NOTE.

Although operating in mid 1942, incorrect recognition confused it with DINAH for some time. Used mostly in Central and S.W. Pacific in small numbers. Little has been seen of the reconnaissance version. This would probably be unarmed forward; solid nose being replaced by small glazed portion; more glazing aft.

In one fighter version, ingenious neat twin tandem turrets are mounted in unglazed rear portion of cockpit. Not a particularly satisfactory aircraft as it tends to have little manoeuvrability. Prototype had opposite rotating propellers which were scrapped in the production model.

Unlikely to be confused with any Allied aircraft. Compare with DINAH and NICK.

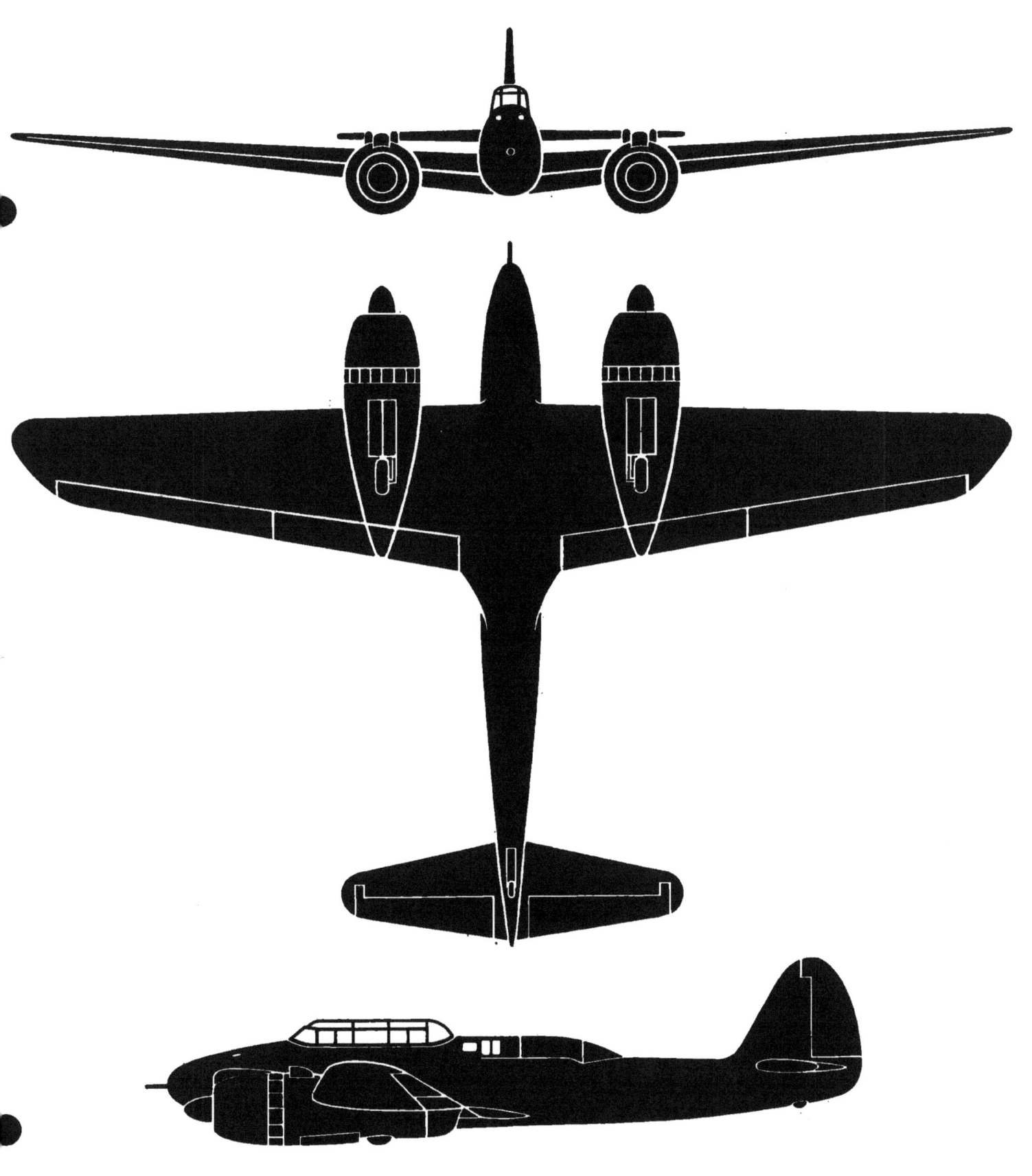

# "NICK"

## ARMY 2. TWIN ENGINED NIGHT AND DAY FIGHTER

CHARACTERISTICS.

A low wing monoplane with dihedral from roots of narrow much tapered and pointed wings.

Two large underslung engines, well streamlined with large spinners.

Short solid nose, slightly longer than engines, raised cabin ending just aft of wing roots, otherwise long slim fuselage ending in point behind tail unit.

Large round topped fin/rudder, wide spanned pointed tailplane.

CREW.
   2.

DIMENSIONS.
   Span 49'6". Length 34'5".

SPEED.
   Maximum.  320 knots at 17,000 feet.
             270 knots at sea level.

OPERATIONAL RADIUS.
   Maximum.  450 miles at 180 knots at 13,000 feet.

BOMB LOAD.
   2 x 30, 50, or 100 kg. bombs (68, 110 or 220 lb) one at each wing root. Bombs may be replaced by long range fuel tanks.

ARMAMENT.
   1 x 20 mm. cannon; or
   2 x 12.7 mm. machine guns  } in top of Nose; and
   1 x 37 mm. cannon underslung offset to starboard; and
   1 x 7.7 mm. machine gun in after Cockpit; or

   1 x 37 mm. cannon in Nose (18 or 25 rounds, 100 r.p.m.).
   1 x 20 mm. cannon in floor of Nose (50 rounds drums).
   1 x 7.7 mm. machine gun in after Cockpit.

NOTE.

Used mainly as aerodrome defence night fighter, possibly as intruder or for ground or shipping attack. First positively identified in mid 1942, since which time it has been used only in small numbers, rarely more than six being over a particular target at one time.

Compare with IRVING and DINAH.

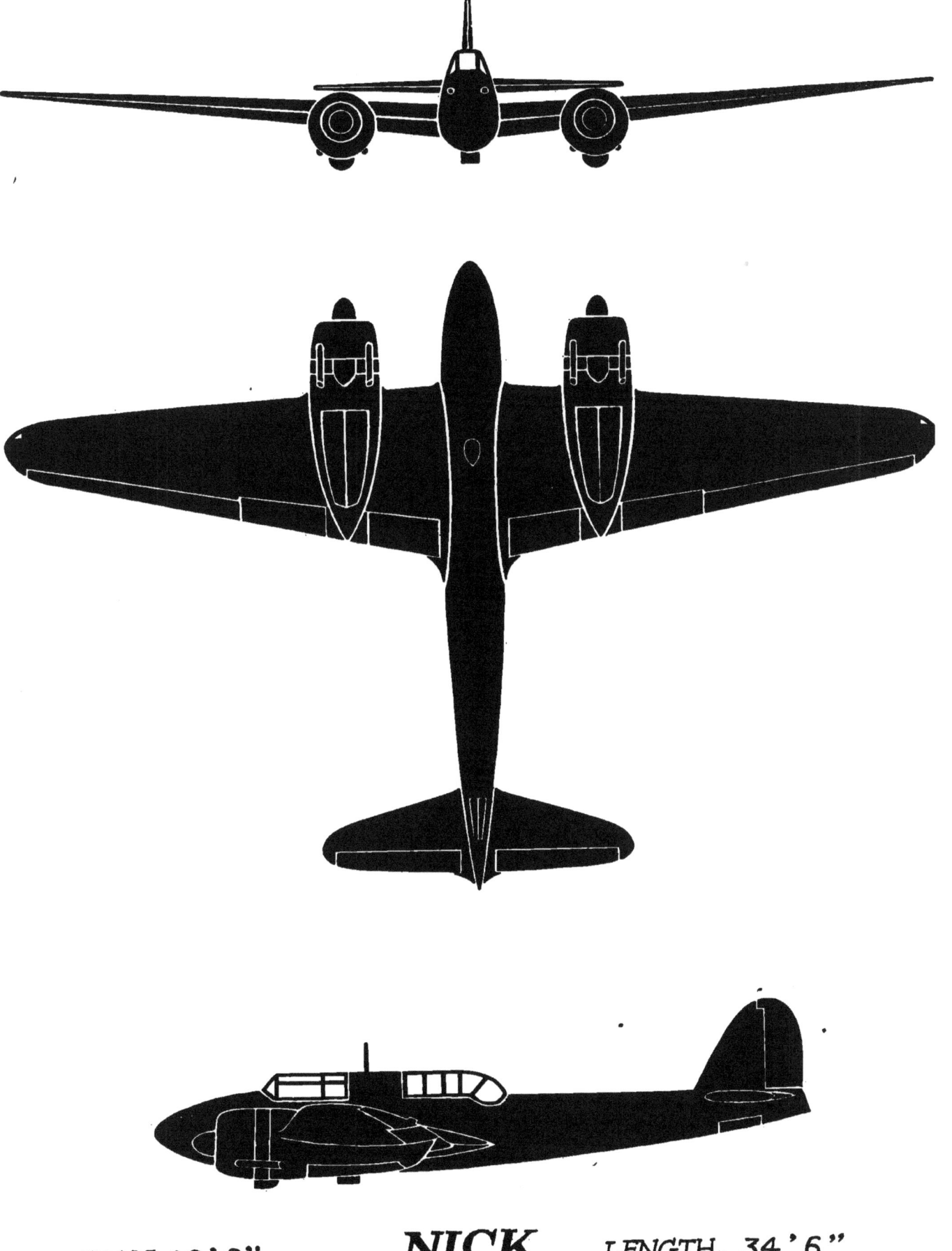

SPAN 37'6" (35-7)    **OSCAR**    LENGTH 29' 8"
SINGLE SEAT FIGHTER

Eastern Fleet Chart Production Unit,

# "OSCAR"

## ARMY 1. SINGLE ENGINED SINGLE SEATER FIGHTER

CHARACTERISTICS.

Low wing monoplane with dihedral from roots. Almost straight leading edge, marked taper on trailing edge, round *or* blunt tips. (Blunt tipped version has shorter span.)

Small radial engine in short cowling.

Long, very slim and tapering fuselage with small cockpit placed far forward.

Small tail unit, triangular fin/rudder. Curved trailing edge. Narrow tapered tail plane.

CREW.

1.

DIMENSIONS.

Span 37'6" or 35'7". Length 29'8".

SPEED.

Maximum. 305 knots at 18,000 feet.
255 knots at sea level.

OPERATIONAL RADIUS.

Maximum. 860 miles with two drop tanks (at 190 knots at 18,000 feet).
580 miles normal.

BOMB LOAD.

Only in blunt wing tipped version; probably up to 2 × 100 kg. (225 lb) bombs or containers of ⅓ kg. bombs for air to air attack.

ARMAMENT.

2 × 12.7 mm. machine guns in Engine Cowling.

NOTE.

A very manœuvrable fighter, its low diving speed, due largely to its light weight, *i.e.*, low wing loading—makes it an easy prey for the heavier Allied fighters. It is vulnerable as tanks are little protected and there is an apparent structural weakness in the fuselage, causing it to crumple during violent manœuvres. The blunt tipped model is the one mostly in current use and has been used as dive bomber. This use will probably increase. Slow speed manœuvrability often offsets advantages of Allied fighter's superior performance.

The very slim long fuselage of OSCAR (emphasised in the blunt tipped version by the shorter span) and the marked trailing edge taper make confusion with Allied types difficult.

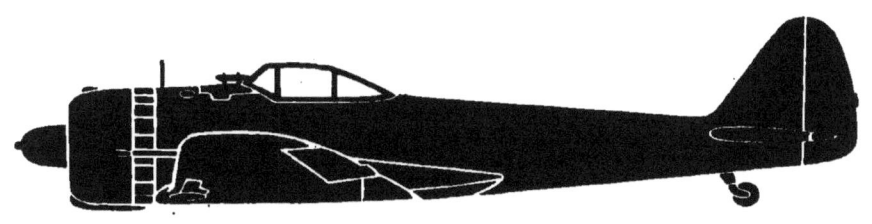

SPAN 37'6" (35-7). **OSCAR** LENGTH 29' 8"

SINGLE SEAT FIGHTER

*Interim Silhouette*
**AR. SCHOOL,
TRINCOMALEE**
*Eastern Fleet Issue*

Eastern Fleet Chart Production Unit.

SPAN 39' 5"  **RUFE**  LENGTH 33' 9"
SINGLE SEAT FIGHTER

# "RUFE"

## NAVY 2. SINGLE ENGINED CENTRAL FLOAT FIGHTER

CHARACTERISTICS.

Low wing monoplane with very marked dihedral from roots of long round tipped wings. Stabilising floats inset from wing tips.

Small radial engine.

Slim fuselage with large central float, attached by thick and two thin struts, projecting well ahead of engine.

Tall triangular fin/rudder. Large tailplane set forward of rudder—small anti-spin fairing below fin/rudder.

CREW.

1.

DIMENSIONS.

Span 39'5". Length 33'9".

SPEED.

Maximum 240 knots at 6,500 feet.
200 knots at sea level.

OPERATIONAL RADIUS.

Maximum 750 miles as reconnaissance fighter.

BOMB LOAD.

2 × 60 kg. (132 lb) bombs may possibly be carried.

ARMAMENT.

2 × 7.7 mm. machine guns over Engine.
2 × 20 mm. cannons in Wings.

NOTE.

Really a ZEKE on floats, RUFE has been modified by the removal of the orginal fuselage point and by the great increase in dihedral. Used as a coastal reconnaissance fighter, RUFE is speedy and manoeuvrable, but is really only of secondary importance, though still a potential enemy of M.T.B.s and small craft.

New faster types will probably replace RUFE in the near future. (NORM: See Section on NEW AIRCRAFT.)

KINGFISHER's deep stubby fuselage, with cockpit merged into it just forward of large tail fin, help to distinguish it from RUFE, together with KINGFISHER's slower speed.

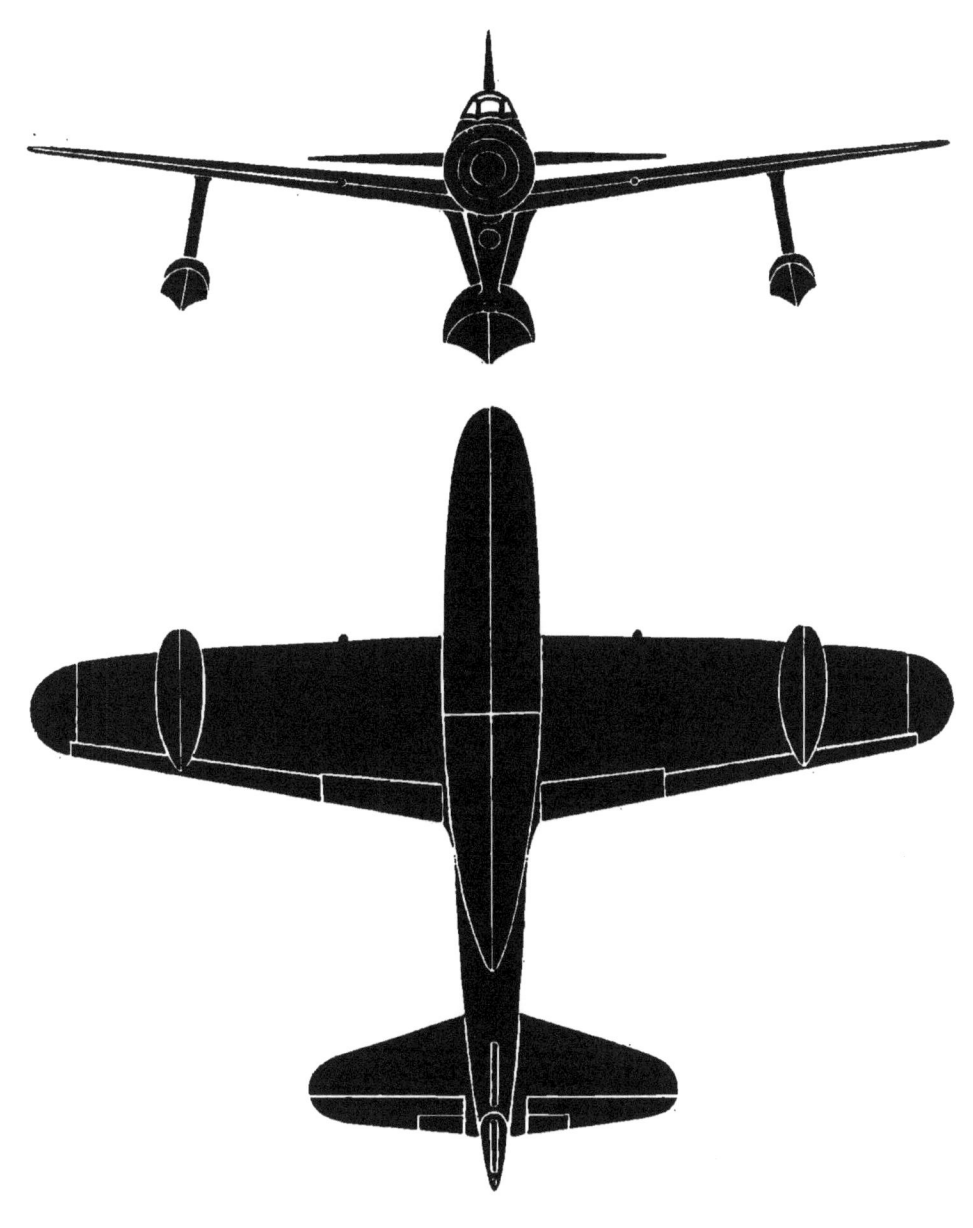

SPAN 39' 5"  **RUFE**  LENGTH 33' 9"
SINGLE SEAT FIGHTER

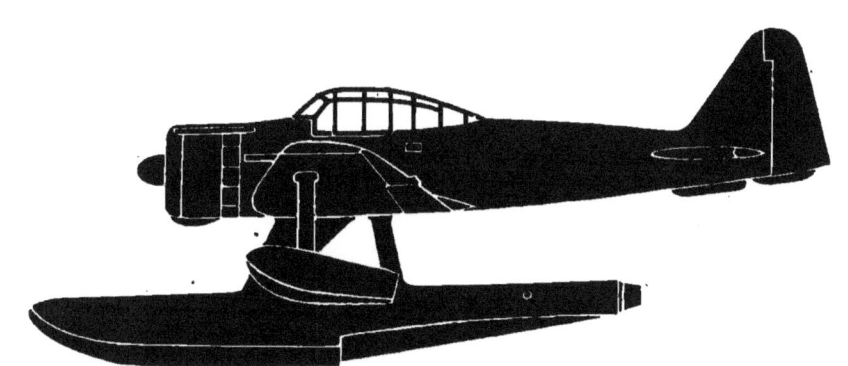

SPAN 31' 0"  **TOJO** II  LENGTH 29' 3"
SINGLE SEAT FIGHTER

Eastern Fleet Chart Production Unit

## "TOJO"

### ARMY 2. SINGLE ENGINED SINGLE SEAT FIGHTER

CHARACTERISTICS.

A low-wing monoplane with dihedral from roots of very short thick wing. Trailing edge has broken taper giving semi-elliptical appearance. Leading edge practically straight.

Large radial engine in short oval cowling.

Fat fuselage tapering quickly to tail unit.

Small tail unit, leading edge of fin very raked, narrow tail plane set far forward of curved rudder.

CREW.

1.

DIMENSIONS.

Span 31'0". Length 29'3".

SPEED.

Maximum 325 knots at 17,00 feet.
260 knots at sea level.

OPERATIONAL RADIUS.

Maximum 675 miles with long range fuel tank.
450 miles normal (at 240 knots at 17,000 feet).

BOMB LOAD.

Unknown at present but as either one central or two wing drop tanks can be carried, bombs are still possibilities.

ARMAMENT.

2 × 7.7 mm. or 2 × 12.7 mm. machine gun in Cowling.
2 × 12.7 mm. machine guns in Wings.

NOTE.

A small, very fast climbing fighter with high ceiling. With a much higher wing loading compared with OSCAR or ZEKE, TOJO's manœuvrability is not exceptional, but it has the highest performance of any Japanese fighter operating in any numbers. Even so some of the new types dealt with in the last Section will replace it eventually.

Little or no fuel tank protection is fitted, and TOJO is prone to explode in the air when hit.

TOJO's small size and short low wings differentiate it from enormous P.47 THUNDERBOLT which is low-mid wing, and has tall pointed fin/rudder.

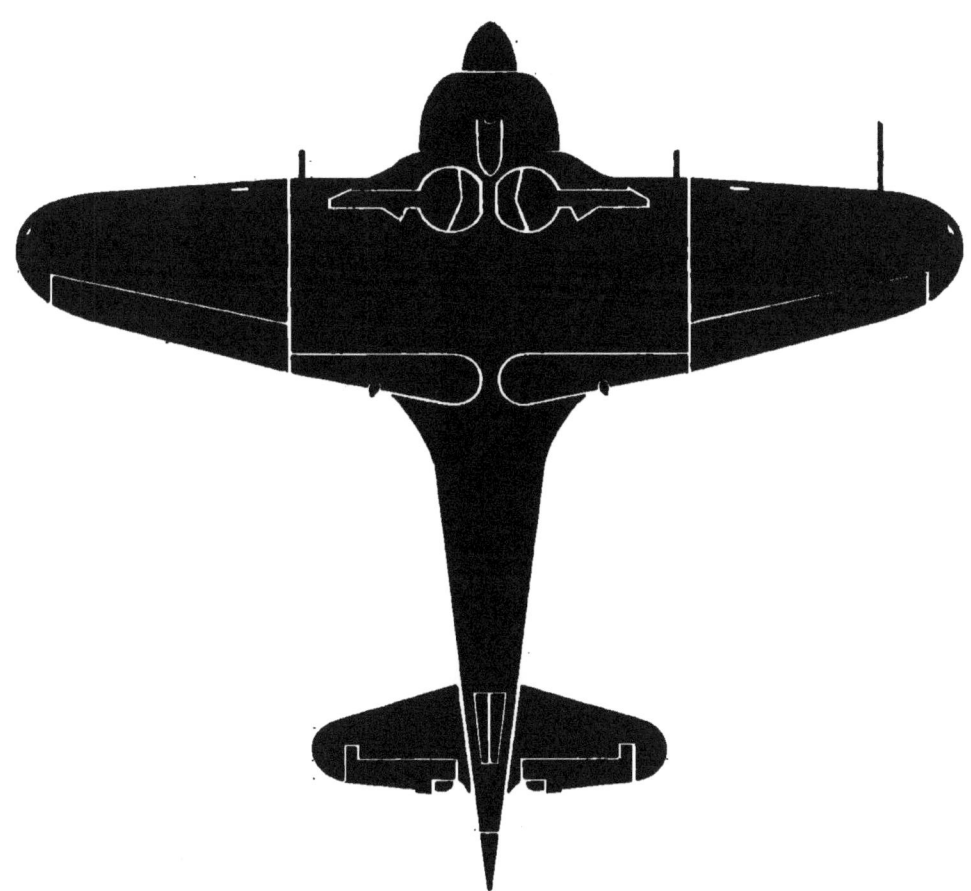

SPAN 31' 0"  **TOJO** II  LENGTH 29' 3"
SINGLE SEAT FIGHTER

Interim Silhouette
*A.R. SCHOOL,*
*TRINCOMALEE.*
*Eastern Fleet Issue.*

Eastern Fleet Chart Production Unit.

SPAN 39'6"  **TONY**  LENGTH 29'6"
SINGLE SEAT FIGHTER

Eastern Fleet Chart Production Unit.

# "TONY"

## ARMY 3. SINGLE IN-LINE ENGINED SINGLE SEAT FIGHTER

CHARACTERISTICS.

Low-wing monoplane with dihedral from roots of long, narrow, round tipped wings.

Long pointed down curved nose—in line engine.

Fuselage slim with curved back; flattish belly broken by large central radiator.

Pointed single fin/rudder. Small tailplane tapered mostly on leading edge.

CREW.

1.

DIMENSIONS.

Span 39'6". Length 29'6".

SPEED.

Maximum 315 knots at 17,000 feet.
250 knots at sea level.

OPERATIONAL RADIUS.

Maximum 650 miles with two drop tanks (at 150 knots at 17,000 feet).
400 miles normal.

BOMB LOAD.

2 × 100 kg. (225 lb) bombs, or
2 × 50 kg. (110 lb) bombs

Carried under wings at half span and replaceable by drop tanks.

ARMAMENT.

4 × 12.7 mm. machine guns (two over Engine and one in each Wing), or
2 × 12.7 mm. machine guns over Engines.
2 × 20 mm. cannon—one in each Wing.

NOTE.

The first modern Army Fighter in service with an in line engine. This is a Japanese version of the inverted V Daimler Benz 601, giving about 1,200 h.p. Designed as a Bomber-destroyer, TONY was probably the first Fighter in service designed with armour built in and is the most heavily armoured Japanese Fighter in current use.

TONY's long narrow wings and down curved nose (due to the inverted V engine with the propellor shaft low down) and small tail unit, differ greatly from the Hurricane's flat broad wings, upswept nose, deep humped fuselage and large tail surfaces.

SPAN 39'6"  **TONY**  LENGTH 29'6"
SINGLE SEAT FIGHTER

Eastern Fleet Chart Production Unit.

*Interim Silhouette*
**A.R. SCHOOL,
TRINCOMALEE**
*Eastern Fleet Issue.*

SPAN 39' 5"  **ZEKE 22**  LENGTH 29' 9"
SINGLE SEAT FIGHTER

Eastern Fleet Chart Production Unit.

# "ZEKE"

## NAVY 0. SINGLE ENGINED CARRIER BORNE FIGHTER

CHARACTERISTICS.

Low-wing monoplane with long tapered round tipped wings and with dihedral from roots.

Small radial engine, well streamlined into fuselage.

Fuselage neatly streamlined with curved belly ending in point behind tail unit and relatively large cockpit set well forward.

Large triangular fin/rudder and wide tail plane set well forward of fuselage point.

CREW.

1.

DIMENSIONS.

Span 39'5". ZEKE 22. Length 29'9".
Span 36'1". ZEKE 52. Length 29'9".

SPEED.

Maximum. 295 knots at 16,000 feet.
250 knots at sea level.

OPERATIONAL RADIUS.

Maximum for reconnaissance 650 miles with long range tank.
Normal 300/350 miles.

BOMB LOAD.

May carry 10 × 32 kg. (68 lb) air burst bombs. 5 under each wing.
Long range fuel tank, central, or two wing tanks may be carried in place of bombs. They are usually dropped if action is joined.

ARMAMENT.

2 × 7.7 mm. machine guns over Engine.
2 × 20 mm. cannons in Wings.

NOTE.

This famous "Zero" Fighter is largely land based, so will be found anywhere on enemy held coasts. Despite its age, with several improvements it is still in considerable production. The more common type in use, ZEKE 22, is roughly the original model with a larger and more powerful engine and folding wing tips for stowage on carriers. The latest model is ZEKE Model 52 which has a shorter span 36'1" and no folding wing tips. This is replacing ZEKE 22. ZEKE's light weight, due to her light construction and, until recently, to her absence of armour, makes it dangerous for fighters engaging her in slow speed manœuvres, since the faster but heavier Allied fighters tend to stall at speeds when ZEKE is most manœuvrable, which is particularly in slow speed climbs.

Radial engine and round tipped extremities make it difficult to compare it with any Allied Fighters yet operating against it. CORSAIR has cranked wing.

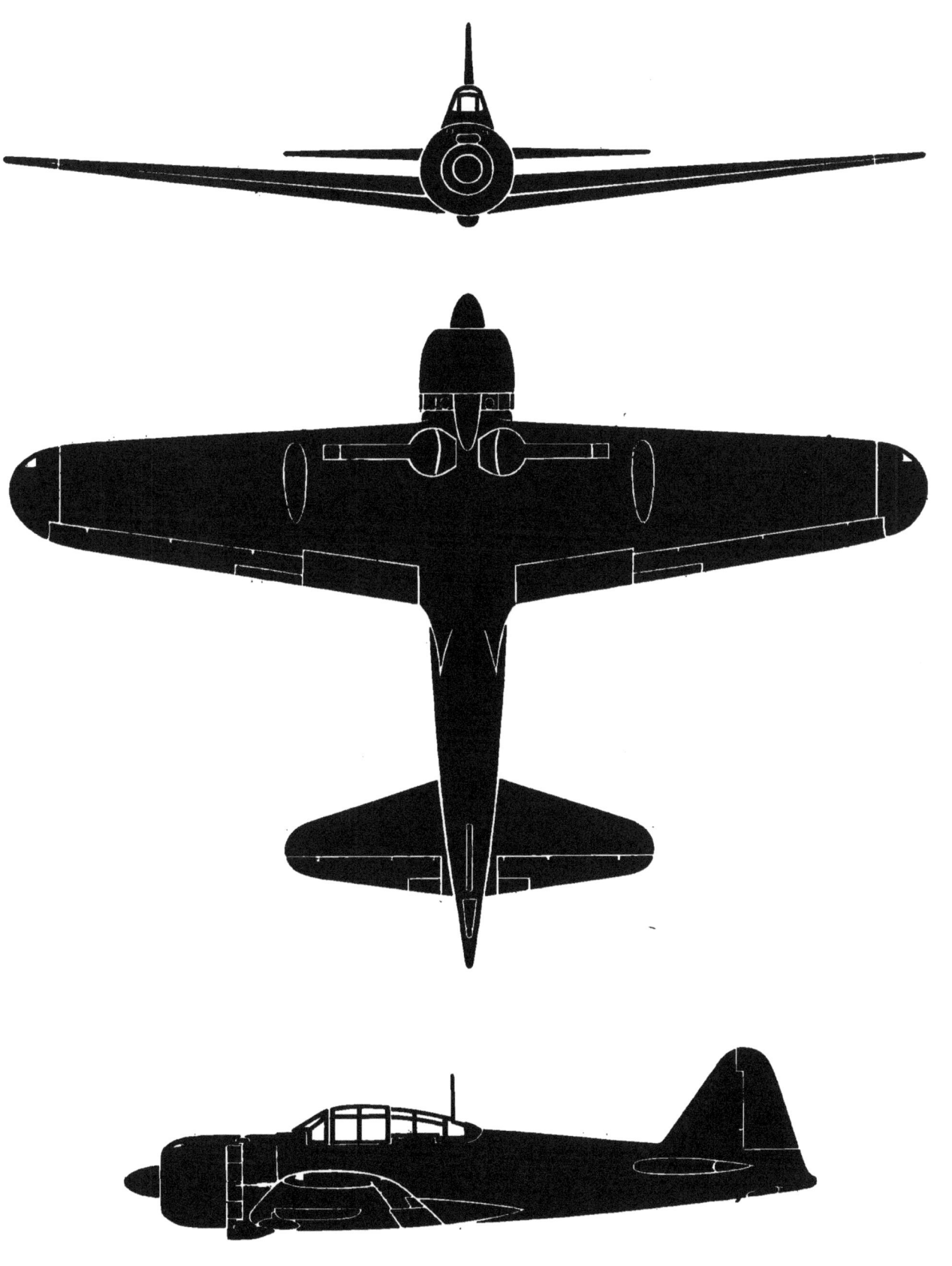

SPAN 36'2"  **ZEKE 32**  LENGTH 29'9"
SINGLE SEAT FIGHTER
(EX HAMP)

Eastern Fleet Chart Production Unit.

# "ZEKE 32" (Ex "HAMP")

## NAVY 0. SINGLE ENGINED CARRIER BORNE FIGHTER

CHARACTERISTICS.

Low-wing monoplane with dihedral from roots of short square tipped wings.

Small radial engine, short nose, well streamlined into fuselage.

Fuselage neatly streamlined, with curved belly, ending in point behind tail unit and relatively large cockpit set well forward.

Large triangular fin/rudder and wide tail plane set well forward of fuselage point.

CREW.
1.

DIMENSIONS.
Span 36'2". Length 29'9".

SPEED.
Maximum 285 knots at 16,000 feet.
250 knots at sea level.

OPERATIONAL RADIUS.
Maximum 650 miles.
Normal 330 miles.

BOMB LOAD.
2 × 30 kg. (68 lb) air burst bombs may be carried at wing roots for use against Allied bombers.

ARMAMENT.
2 × 20 mm. cannon in wings.
2 × 7.7 mm. machine guns in engine cowling.

NOTE.

HAMP is really a modification of ZEKE with the folding wing tips removed to increase speed by reduction of frictional resistance. This increases speed and manoeuvrability. It is slowly being replaced by the short spanned, round wing tipped version ZEKE MODEL 52 and is itself out of production. The large tail unit, the size of which is emphasised by the reduced wing span, is a very notable feature. To conform with the new nomenclature the name HAMP is to be dropped and in future will be known as ZEKE 32.

Compare with MARTLET and HELLCAT; both having square cut tail fin/rudder and tail planes and both deep stubby, mid wing fighters, with angular lines—the latter also having a flat centre section before dihedral begins.

SPAN 36'2" **ZEKE 32** LENGTH 29'9"
SINGLE SEAT FIGHTER
(EX HAMP)

Interim Silhouette
A.R. SCHOOL,
TRINCOMALEE
Eastern Fleet Issue

Eastern Fleet Chart Production Unit.

SPAN 36' 1"  **ZEKE 52**  LENGTH 29' 9"
SINGLE SEAT FIGHTER

Eastern Fleet Chart Production Unit.

SPAN 36' 1"  **ZEKE 52**  LENGTH 29' 9"
SINGLE SEAT FIGHTER

Interim Silhouette
R. SCHOOL,
TRINCOMALEE
Eastern Fleet Issue

# NEW AIRCRAFT

## TRENDS IN JAPANESE DEVELOPMENT, AND NEW AIRCRAFT

For some months, information has been accumulating about the Japanese production of engines of the 2000 horse power class. It has been obvious too, that many existing airframes could not take engines of that power and that consequently new types, both fighter and bombers, were to be expected. Some of these aircraft have already been in action and preliminary silhouettes and a few photographs are included in this handbook (Frances, Jill, Judy and Liz). Others are known to be either in advanced experimental stages or first production, but of these there is insufficient information available to compile reasonable silhouettes and little or no photographic cover. These, then, are not included but will be as soon as adequate detail arrives. They have, however, been allotted code-names and a list of thirteen new aircraft is appended with brief details, and in two cases line drawings.

FIGHTERS.

*Navy.*

|  |  | *Remarks* |
|---|---|---|
| George. | Single radial engine, 18 cyls. 2000 h.p. | In production. |
| Jack. | Single radial engine, 14 cyls. |  |
| Rex. | Single radial engine, float fighter. | In production, probably will replace Rufe. |
| Sam. | Single radial engine, carrier borne. | 25—30 mm. wing guns reported. |

*Army.*

| Frank. | Single radial engine, 18 cyls. 2000 h.p. | Probably in production. |
| Pat. | Single in line engine. | Reported "as very high speed long range." |
| Rob. | Single in line engine (Jap. version of D.B.603?). | Very pointed nose. |
| Steve. | Single radial engine, 18 cyls. 2000 h.p. | "Super high speed." |

RECONNAISSANCE.

*Navy.*

| Norm. | Single radial engine float plane. | High speed. |
| Paul. | Single radial engine, float plane. | Probably used as dive bomber so twin floats are likely. |
| Myrtle. | Single radial engine, deck landing. | Several sightings already in S.W.P. and C.P. Areas. |

*Army.*

| Clara. | Twin radial engines 18 cyls. 2000 h.p. | Ultimately replacing Dinah. |
| Edna. | Twin radial engines 14 cyls. |  |

Except for Frances no really new bomber is sufficiently well known to have been given a code-name, but these new aircraft, including Frances, Jill, Judy and Liz, represent the main trend in aircraft production in Japan—namely long range anti-shipping dive and torpedo bombers, single and multi-engined, and fighters of great fire power and a high rate of climb, but short range. These latter are designated Kyokuchi or "vital-area-defence" fighters and together with the anti shipping bombers, are designed to take care of each phase to be expected in a combined assault on the Japanese Islands, by high altitude bombers and an invasion fleet, though all will probably be used in other theatres first.

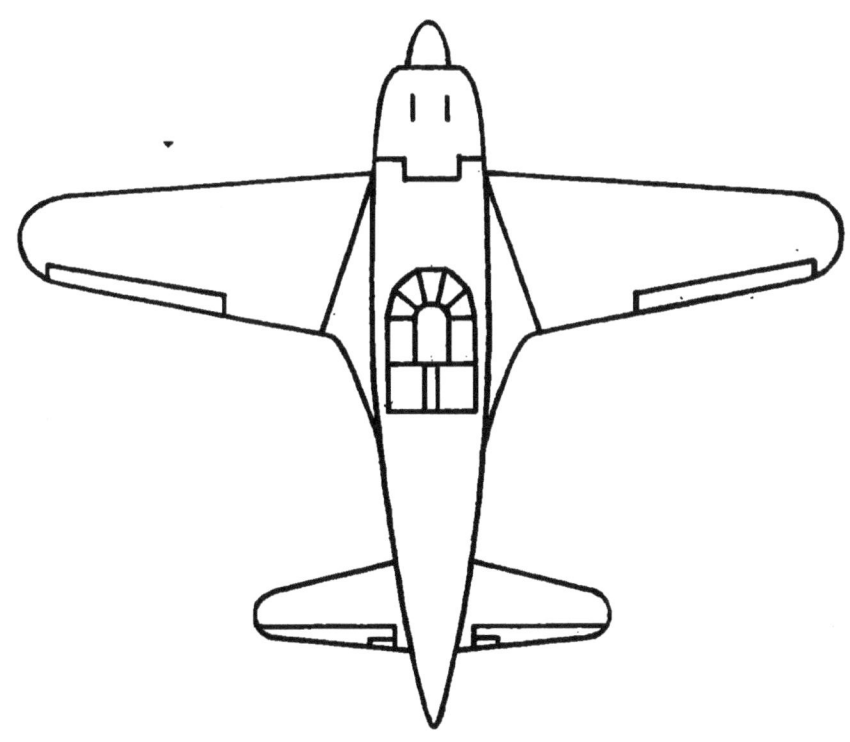

SPAN 35' 5"  **JACK**  LENGTH 31' 10"

*Interim Silhouete*
*A.R. SCHOOL*
*TRINCOMALEE*
*Eastern Fleet Issue*

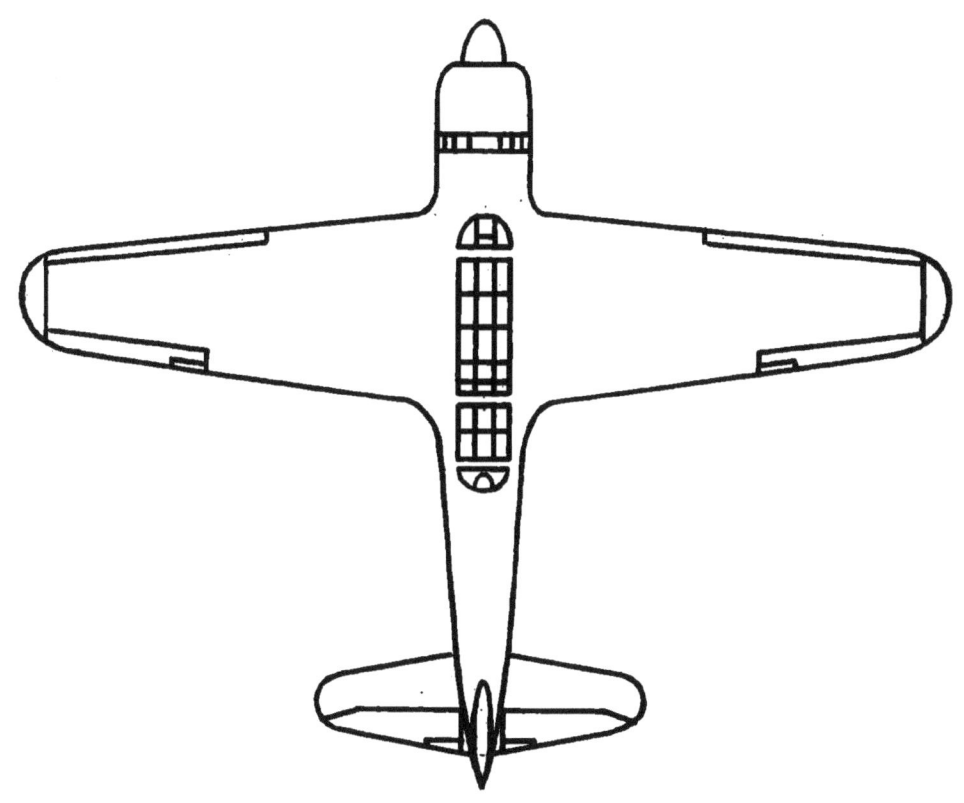

SPAN 41' 2"  **MYRTLE**  LENGTH 36" 6'

*Interim Silhouette*
*A.R. SCHOOL,*
*TRINCOMALEE*
*Eastern Fleet Issue*

Produced by Eastern Fleet Chart Production Unit.

It is known that several twin or four engined bombers are likely to appear, but as both Army and Navy are constantly improving existing designs, equipping them where possible with the larger engines as they become available, it is probable that fewer bombers than fighters will appear.

Amongst the improvements are the conversion of some Army light bombers, *e.g.*, LILY, to dive bomber, and the carrying of bombs by most Army fighters—all with a view to converting every suitable type into a multi-use aircraft. This, of course, is a parallel of the War in the West during the latter part of 1943.

More details are known of three of the KYOKUCHI fighters listed above, namely JACK, GEORGE and FRANK and a line drawing of JACK taken from a captured official manual is included in this section. A similar line drawing of MYRTLE is also included.

From previous experience with Japanese recognition drawings, several inaccuracies are to be expected, but basically it should prove correct and suffice until a silhouette can be drawn from captured or crashed specimens.

1. JACK. Navy fighter. Armament will almost certainly be $4 \times 20$ mm. cannons. Rate of climb is reported to be 29,580 feet in $14\frac{1}{2}$ minutes. This plane is in production and in limited operation. Speed 355 knots at 20,000 feet; 305 knots at sea level. Op. radius 250—325 miles.

2. GEORGE. Navy fighter. Known to be in operation. It carries $4 \times 20$ mm. cannons though originally intended to have an extra $2 \times 7.7$ mm. machine guns. It has a top speed of 325 knots.

3. FRANK. Army fighter. Thought to be an improvement on TOJO, it has a top speed of 355 knots and a rate of climb of 29,500 feet in $19\frac{1}{2}$ minutes. Armament is expected to be $2 \times 37$ mm. and $4 \times 20$ mm. cannons, but this has yet to be confirmed and will probably be less. The all up weight is nearly 8,000 lb.

These figures confirm the idea that the Naval types would not normally operate from carriers as their high speed and high all up weight would make landings hazardous, and their short range necessitate the carriers operating embarrassingly close to the Allied attacking force.

4. MYRTLE. Navy reconnaissance. At first thought to be a modified JILL with longer nose. Capture of several, show her to be a smaller aircraft. Span 41'3". Length 36'5". A three seater, the central cockpit is for the camera operator/observer. Performance figures uncertain yet, but the aircraft is fast (about 340 knots maximum) and manœuvrable.

NOTE.—As more information on these new aircraft is collected, amendments to this section will be produced, until sufficient is known for a complete set of data and photographs to be included in the appropriate section.

www.ingramcontent.com/pod-product-compliance
Lightning Source LLC
Chambersburg PA
CBHW061056170426
43193CB00025B/2989